SpeakEasy Spanish™

SURVIVAL SPANISH

FOR

CUSTOMER SERVICE

Myelita Melton, MA

SpeakEasy Communications, Incorporated

Survival Spanish for Customer Service

Author: Myelita A. Melton
Cover Design: Ellen Wass Beckerman

Published by SpeakEasy Communications, Incorporated
116 Sea Trail Drive
Mooresville, NC 28117-8493
USA

ISBN 10:   0-9786998-1-5
ISBN 13:   978-0-97869981-9

Survival Spanish for Customer Service, SpeakEasy Spanish, SpeakEasy's Survival Spanish, SpeakEasy's Survival Spanish for Customer Service, and SpeakEasySpanish.com are either trademarks or registered trademarks of SpeakEasy Communications, Inc. in the United States and/or other countries.

The content of this book is furnished for informational use only, is subject to change without notice, and should not be construed as a commitment by SpeakEasy Communications, Incorporated. SpeakEasy Communications, Incorporated assumes no responsibility or liability for any errors, omissions, or inaccuracies that may appear in the informational content contained in this guide.

Survival Spanish for Customer Service
Table of Contents

Using This Material

Welcome to *SpeakEasy's Survival Spanish for Customer Service*. This material is for adults with no previous experience in the Spanish language. Through research and interviews with customer service professionals in a variety of fields, we have developed this material to be a practical guide for using Spanish on the job. Wherever possible, we have chosen to use the similarities between English and Spanish to facilitate your success.

Throughout the manual you will find study tips and pronunciation guides that will help you to say the words correctly. In the guides, we have broken down the Spanish words for you by syllables, choosing English words that closely approximate the Spanish sound needed. This method makes learning Spanish more accessible because it doesn't seem so foreign. When you see letters that are **BOLD** in the guide, say that part of the word the loudest. The bold capital letters are there to show you where the emphasis falls in that word.

At SpeakEasy Communications, we believe that *communication* is more important than *conjugation*, and that what you learn must be practical for what you do. We urge you to set realistic, practical goals. Make practice a regular part of your day and you will be surprised at the progress you make!

SpeakEasy's Secrets to Learning Spanish

Congratulations on your decision to learn Spanish! This decision is one of the smartest choices you will ever make considering the increasing diversity in our country. It's definitely one you will never regret. You are now among a growing number of America's visionary leaders, who want to build more trusting relationships with Hispanic-Americans, the fastest growing segment of our population.

Learning Spanish is going to open many doors for you, and it will affect you in ways you can't imagine. By learning Spanish, you will be able to work more efficiently and safely in almost every workplace in the nation. Since bilingual employees are currently in short supply nationwide, you will find increasing job opportunities in almost every profession. In addition, you will be able to build stronger relationships with Latinos you meet anywhere you go. There's also another added benefit: You are going to raise your communication skills to a whole new level.

As an adult, learning a new language requires a certain mind set. It takes time, patience and more than a little stubbornness. Think about it. You didn't learn English overnight. You began crying as an infant. That was your first attempt at communication. Later you uttered syllables. When you did, your parents thought you were the world's smartest child, and they rewarded you constantly. After a few years you began to make simple sentences. By the time you reached your first class in school, if you were like me, you couldn't stop talking. So, you can't expect to know everything about Spanish by studying it for only a few weeks. You must give Spanish time to sink in just like English did.

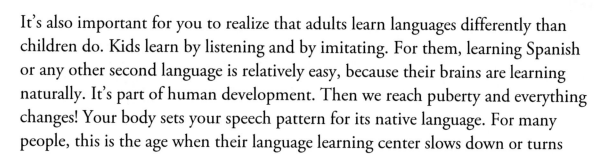

It's also important for you to realize that adults learn languages differently than children do. Kids learn by listening and by imitating. For them, learning Spanish or any other second language is relatively easy, because their brains are learning naturally. It's part of human development. Then we reach puberty and everything changes! Your body sets your speech pattern for its native language. For many people, this is the age when their language learning center slows down or turns completely off. Your body just figures it doesn't need it anymore. Coincidentally, this slow-down occurs about the time that you hit your seventh grade Spanish class. That's why learning Spanish seemed to be so hard—that, and the huge

amount of very impractical things you were forced to learn. As a result of this physical change in puberty, adults tend to learn languages more visually. Listening and imitating are still important; especially when paired with a visual cue. Most adults benefit from seeing a Spanish word spelled phonetically and hearing it at the same time. This combination helps your brain make sense of the new sounds.

Adults are also practical learners. If you see a reason for what you are learning, you will find it easier to accomplish. It is very true that if you practice your Spanish daily, you are less likely to lose it. Yes, you can teach an old dog new tricks! You are *never* too old to learn Spanish.

If you did take Spanish in high school or college, you are going to be pleasantly surprised when words and phrases you thought you had forgotten begin to come back to you. That previous experience with other languages is still in your mind. It's just hidden away in a little-used filing cabinet. Soon that cabinet will open up again and that's going to help you learn new words even faster.

Here's another thought you should consider. *What they told you in the traditional foreign language classroom was not exactly correct.* There's no such thing as *"perfect Spanish"* just as there is no *"perfect English."* This fact leaves the door for good communication wide open!

The secret to learning Spanish is having *self-confidence and a great sense of humor*. To build self-confidence, you must realize that the entire learning experience is painless and fun. Naturally, you are going to make mistakes. Everyone does. We all make mistakes in English too! So get ready to laugh and learn. *Don't think that you have to have a perfect Spanish sentence in your head before you say something.* It's very important for you to say what you know—even if it's only a word or two. The point is to communicate. Communication doesn't have to be "pretty" or perfect to be effective.

Español is one of the world's most precise and expressive languages. Consider these other important facts as you begin to "*habla español*":

- ✓ English and Spanish share a common Latin heritage, so literally thousands of words in our two languages are either *similar* or *identical*.

- ✓ Your ability to communicate is the most important thing, so your grammar and pronunciation don't have to be "*perfect*" for you to be understood.

- ✓ Some very practical and common expressions in Spanish can be communicated with a few simple words.

- ✓ As the number of Latinos in the United States increases, so do your opportunities to practice. Saying even a phrase or two in Spanish every day will help you learn faster.

- ✓ Relax! People who enjoy their learning experiences acquire Spanish at a much faster pace than others.

- ✓ Set realistic goals and establish reasonable practice habits.

- ✓ When you speak even a little Spanish, you are showing a tremendous respect for the Hispanic culture and its people.

- ✓ Even a little Spanish or *poco español* goes a long way!

As you begin the process of learning Spanish, you are going to notice a few important differences. Speaking Spanish is going to feel and sound a little odd to you at first. This feeling is completely normal because you are using muscles in your face that English doesn't require, and your inner ear is not accustomed to hearing you speak Spanish. People tell me it sounds and feels like a cartoon character has gotten inside your head! Don't let that stop you. Just keep right on going!

Many Americans know more Spanish than they realize and they can pronounce many words perfectly. Review the list below. How many of the Spanish words in it do you recognize? Using what you already know about Spanish will enable you to learn new things easier and faster, and it's a great way to build your confidence.

Amigos Similares y Familiares

Nachos	Amigo	Hospital	Español	Doctor
Loco	Hotel	Oficina	Agua	Fiesta
Burrito	Taco	Olé	No problema	Accidente
Dinero	Salsa	Teléfono	Quesadilla	Margarita
Tequila	Tortilla	Bueno	Grande	Mucho
Sombrero	Adiós	Gracias	Feliz Navidad	Hasta la vista

The Sounds of Spanish

No se preocupe. Don't worry. One of your biggest concerns about acquiring a new language will be speaking it well enough so that others can understand you. Spanish is close enough to English that making a few mistakes along the way won't hurt your ability to communicate.

The most important sounds in Spanish consist of *five* vowels. Each one is pronounced the way it is written. Spanish vowels are never *silent*. Even if there are two vowels together in a word, both of them will stand up and be heard.

A	(ah)	as in mama
E	(eh)	as in "hay or the "eh" in set
I	(ee)	as in deep
O	(oh)	as in open
U	(oo)	as in spoon

Here are the other sounds you'll need to remember. Always pronounce them the same way. Spanish is a very consistent language. The sounds the letters make don't shift around as much as they do in English.

Spanish Letter		English Sound
C	(before an e or i)	s as in Sam: **cero:** SAY-row
G	(before an e or i)	h as in he: **energía:** n-air-HE-ah
		emergencia: a-mare-HEN-see-ah
H		silent: **hacienda:** ah-see-N-da
J		h as in hot: **Julio,** HOO-lee-oh
LL		y as in yoyo: **tortilla,** tor-TEE-ya
Ñ		ny as in canyon: **español,** es-pan-NYOL
QU		k as in kit: **tequila,** tay-KEY-la
RR		The "trilled" r sound: **burro,** BOO-row
V		v as in Victor: **Victor,** Vic-TOR
Z		s as in son: **Gonzales,** gone-SA-les

The Other Consonants: The remaining letters in Spanish have very similar sounds to their equivalents in English.

**Note: People from Latin American countries have a variety of accents just like Americans do. In certain areas of Latin America people tend to pronounce the letter "v" more like the English letter "b." This accent is particularly true in some parts of Mexico. In other Latin American countries a "v" sounds like an English "v." If you learned to switch the "v" sound for a "b" sound in high school or college Spanish classes, don't change your habit; however, if you haven't had any experience with Spanish before now, don't sweat the small stuff! Pronounce the "v" as you normally would.

The Spanish Alphabet
El alfabeto español

A	ah	J	HO-ta	R	AIR-ray
B	bay	K	ka	RR	EH-rray
C	say	L	L-ay	S	S-ay
CH	chay	LL	A-yea	T	tay
D	day	M	M-ay	U	oo
E	A or EH	N	N-ay	V	vay
F	f-ay	Ñ	N-yea	W	DOE-blay-vay
G	hay	O	oh	X	A-kees
H	AH-chay	P	pay	Y	ee-gree-A-gah
I	ee	Q	coo	Z	SAY-ta

Did you notice something different about the Spanish alphabet? It has four letters the English alphabet doesn't have. Can you find them?

The Four "Extra" Letters

Look carefully at the table above which contains the Spanish alphabet. Did you notice that the Spanish language has more letters in its alphabet than English does? There are thirty letters in the Spanish alphabet. Even though Spanish has more letters in its alphabet, none of them will present *problemas* for you. Here are the four extra letters and words in which they are used:

CH   Sounds like the following English words: Chuck, Charlie and Chocolate. Try saying these Spanish words: Nacho and macho

LL   Sounds essentially like an English "y." However, you will hear slight variations depending on where the person is from who is speaking Spanish to you. **Example:** Tortilla (tor-T-ya)

Ñ   Sounds like a combination of "ny" as in canyon or onion:
Example: español (es-pan-**NYOL**)

RR   This letter is a "trilled" sound. Practice by taking your tongue and placing it in the roof of your mouth just behind your front teeth. Blow air across the tip of your tongue to make it flutter. This sound can be difficult to make. It's only strange because you are moving your tongue muscle in a new way. Since there are no words in English with trilled sounds, you never learned to move your tongue that way. Learning how to do it will take time, patience and practice! Don't let a problem with the trilled "r" stop you from speaking. Essentially the sounds of the English "r" and the Spanish "r" are the same. To start with, say the double "r" a bit louder than a single "r." **Example:** Burrito (boo-**REE**-toe)

TIPS & TECHNIQUES
It's normal for English-speaking people to have problems with the trilled "r" sounds in Spanish. Don't sweat the small stuff! With practice you will be able to accomplish this feat! It's something you've never done before, so cut yourself some slack. You will be able to communicate. That's all that matters in survival Spanish.

The Spanish Accent

In Spanish you will see two types of accent marks. Both marks are very important and do different things. One of the marks you will notice is called a "tilde." It is only found over the letter "N." But, don't get the Ñ confused with N. The accent mark over Ñ makes it into a different letter entirely. In fact, it's one of four letters in the Spanish alphabet that the English alphabet doesn't have. The Ñ changes the sound of the letter to a combination of "ny." You'll hear the sound that this important letter makes in the English words "canyon" and "onion."

Occasionally you will see another accent mark over a letter in a Spanish word. The accent mark or "slash" mark shows you where to place vocal emphasis. So, when you see an accent mark over a letter in a Spanish word, just say that part of the word louder. For example: José (ho-**SAY**). These accented syllables are indicated in our pronunciation guides with bold, capital letters.

Pronouncing Spanish Words

The pronunciation of Spanish words follows very basic, consistent rules. This regular pattern makes it easier to learn. Here are some tips to remember:

1. Most Spanish words that end with vowels are stressed or emphasized on the *next to the last* syllable.

    Señorita: sen-your-**REE**-ta   Jalapeño: ha-la-**PAIN**-yo

2. Look for an accent mark. If the Spanish word has an accent in it, that's the emphasized syllable.

    José: ho-**SAY**   ¿Cómo está?: **KO**-mo es-**TA**

3. Words that end in consonants are stressed on the *final* syllable.

    Doctor: doc-**TOR**   Hotel: oh-**TELL**

Spanish Punctuation Marks

Spanish has two different punctuation marks than English does. Both of them are upside down versions of English punctuation marks. They are used to signal you that something other than a simple declarative sentence is just ahead.

First, there's the upside down question mark (¿). You will see it at the beginning of all questions. It's there simply to let you know that what follows is a question and you will need to give your voice an upward inflection. It's the same inflection we use in English.

Example: Do you speak English?   ¿Habla inglés?

Second, there's the upside down exclamation mark (¡). It's there to let you know that what follows should be vocally emphasized.

Example: Hi!   ¡Hola!

8

Spanglish

Much of the southwestern part of the United States originally belonged to Mexico. In 1848, after the US-Mexican War, the border was moved south to the Rio Grande River. The treaty that was signed at the end of the conflict transformed Spanish-speaking Mexicans into Americans overnight! Imagine waking up one morning and finding out that you are a citizen of another country — and that you have to learn a new language! As a result, an entirely new slang language was born that mixes the best of both worlds: *Spanglish*.

In America, Spanglish really started to come into its own in the early 1970s. At that time it gained both in popularity and vocabulary. Now, people who use Spanglish span generations, classes, and nationalities. It's heard in pop music, seen in print, and used in conversations throughout Latin America. It isn't just an American phenomenon. Immigrants may turn to Spanglish out of necessity while they are learning English, and bilingual speakers use it because it's convenient. If you listen to native speakers carefully, you will hear them use a mixture of languages. Sometimes in the middle of a conversation, you may hear an English word or two. People who speak Spanish tend to use whatever word or phrase suits their purpose and is most descriptive. In general conversation it doesn't matter what language it is. Even though Spanglish is still frowned upon in most traditional language classes and by those who want to keep the Spanish language "pure," it really is a great tool for most people.

Common Spanglish Words

Truck = Trocka	Lunch = Lonche	No parking = No parque
Yard = Yarda	Break = Breaka	Cell phone = Cel
Carpet = Carpeta	Check = Chequear	Market = Marketa
Push = Puchar	Roof = Ruffo	Email = Email

More Amigos Familiares

Using what you've learned about how Spanish sounds, practice the words listed below. Examine them carefully. Each word bears a strong resemblance to its English counterpart or it's a common Spanish word many people use who doesn't speak Spanish. Begin by carefully and slowly pronouncing each word on the list. If you have trouble, go back and review the Spanish vowel sounds again. Continue by reviewing the section on Spanish accents and pronunciation. Reviewing these three concepts will help you as you continue building your skills. Practice these similar and familiar words often. They will help you remember the basic, important sounds of *español*.

Accidente	Flan	Padre
Aeropuerto	Flor	Paga
Apartamento	Florería	Patata
Aplicación	Fruta	Persona
Avenida	General	Piña
Banana	Gimnasio	Plato
Banco	Hacienda	Policía
Bueno	Hamburguesa	Posible
Café	Hasta mañana	Progreso
Carro	Identificación	Rápido
Caución	Importante	Restaurante
Centro	Interesante	Río
Chocolate	Jalapeño	Rosbif
Conversación	Jamón	Servicio
Dentista	Leche	Super mercado
Diciembre	Macarrones	Supervisor
Dirección	Mecánico	Té

Muchos Ways to "Practicar"

The more you listen to and use your *español,* the easier it will be to learn it. There are lots of ways to practice, that won't cost you any money. Try these super techniques for improving your skills:

- ✓ Next time you're at a Mexican restaurant, order your food in *español.*

- ✓ Start slowly. Practice one sound each week.

- ✓ Read Spanish language newspapers. They are usually free and easily available.

- ✓ Listen to Spanish language radio stations.

- ✓ Watch Spanish language television.

- ✓ Rent Spanish language videos; especially cartoons.

- ✓ Buy Spanish tapes and listen to them in the car while you commute.

- ✓ And — speaking of tapes, there is such a variety of Latin *música* available, something will be right for you. Listening to music is a great way to train your ears to Spanish and have fun doing it. Personally, I like anything by Carlos Santana or the Salsa of Marc Anthony. What do you like?

- ✓ Visit Internet sites like *www.about.com* or *www.studyspanish.com.* You can find all kinds of information there about the Spanish language. They have a wonderful, free newsletter that comes to you via e-mail. Most search engines have some sort of Spanish section. An on-line search will turn up lots of treasures!

- ✓ Next time you listen to a baseball game, keep track of all the Hispanic names you hear.

- ✓ Speak Spanish every time the opportunity presents itself. Practice is the only way to get over your nervousness.

- ✓ Try to learn with a friend at work and practice together.

What practice habits work for you? Share them with us at:
info@speakeasyspanish.com

SpeakEasy's Tips and Techniques
for Comunicación

It's important to remember, when you're trying to communicate with a person who is "limited in English proficiency," *patience is a virtue*! Put yourself in their shoes and think how you would feel if the roles were reversed. Here are some easy things you can do to make the conversation easier for both of you.

- ✓ Speak slowly and distinctly.

- ✓ Do not use slang expressions or colorful terms.

- ✓ Get straight to the point! Unnecessary words cloud your meaning.

- ✓ Speak in a normal tone. Speaking *loudly* doesn't help anyone understand you any better!

- ✓ Look for cues to meaning in body language and facial expressions. Use gestures of your own to get your point across.

- ✓ You may not receive good eye contact. Do not interpret the lack of eye contact negatively.

- ✓ Latinos tend to stand closer to each other than North Americans do when they talk with each other, so your personal space could feel crowded. Stand your ground!

- ✓ Feel free to use gestures and body language of your own to communicate.

- ✓ Because of the way languages are learned, it is likely that the person you are talking to understands more of what you are saying, than he is able to verbalize. *So, be careful what you say!* No matter what the language, we always understand the bad words first!

Tips & Tidbits

Throughout your book look for the light bulb you see above. This section will give you helpful hints and cultural information designed to help you learn Spanish more easily.

Beginning Words & Phrases

Let's get started! In no time you will start gaining confidence. Your Latino customers and colleagues will be delighted you are learning to speak *español*.

English	Español	Guide
Hi!	¡Hola!	OH-la
How are you?	¿Cómo está?	CO-mo es-TA
Fine	Muy bien.	mooy b-N
So so	Así así	ah-SEE ah-SEE
Bad	Mal	mal
Good morning	Buenos días	boo-WAY-nos D-ahs
Good afternoon	Buenas tardes	boo-WAY-nas TAR-days
Good night	Buenas noches.	boo-WAY-nas NO-chase
Sir or Mister	Señor	sen-YOUR
Mrs. or Ma'am	Señora	sen-YOUR-ah
Miss	Señorita	sen-your- REE-ta
What's your name?	¿Cómo se llama?	CO-mo say YA-ma
My name is ___.	Me llamo ____.	may YA-mo
Nice to meet you.	¡Mucho gusto!	MOO-cho GOO-stow
Thank you.	Gracias.	GRA-see-ahs
Please!	¡Por favor!	pour-fa-VOR
You're welcome.	De nada.	day NA da
The pleasure is mine.	El gusto es mío.	el GOO-stow es ME-oh
I'm sorry.	Lo siento.	low-see-N-toe
Excuse me.	¡Perdón!	pear-DON
Good-bye	Adiós	ah-dee-OS

Spanish Sounds Rápido—What Do I Do Now?

Be honest! One of the reasons you are hesitant to speak Spanish is that it sounds so fast! Naturally, you're afraid you won't understand. Here are some phrases that will help you. Make learning them a priority. *¿Comprende, amigo?*

English	Español	Guide
I don't understand.	No comprendo.	no com-**PREN**-doe
Do you understand?	¿Comprende?	com-**PREN**-day
I speak a little Spanish.	Hablo poco español.	**AH**-blow **POE**-co es-pan-**NYOL**
Do you speak English?	¿Habla inglés?	**AH**-bla eng-**LACE**
Repeat, please.	Repita, por favor.	ray-**PETE**-ah pour fa-**VOR**
I'm studying Spanish.	Estudio español.	es-**TOO**-d-oh es-pan-**NYOL**
Write it, please	Escribe, por favor.	es-**SCRE**-bay pour fa-**VOR**
Speak more slowly.	Habla más despacio.	**AH**-bla mas des-**PA**-see-oh
Thanks for your patience.	Gracias por su paciencia.	**GRA**-see-ahs pour sue pa-see-**N**-see-ah
How do you say it in Spanish?	¿Cómo se dice en español?	**CO**-mo say **DEE**-say n es-pan-**NYOL**
Where are you from?	¿De dónde es?	day **DON**-day es
May I help you?	¿Puedo ayudarle?	pooh-**A**-doe eye-you-**DAR**-lay

The key here is not to pánico.
Your Spanish-speaking employee or friend is having just as much trouble understanding you, as you are having understanding them! Hang in there! Between the two of you *comunicación* will begin to take place.

14

For Practice—Para Practicar

Practice Conversation I

USTED (YOU):   Good morning, Sir.

SR. GARCÍA   Good morning. How are you?

USTED   Fine, thanks. How are you?

SR. GARCÍA   OK, thanks.

Practice Conversation II

USTED: May I help you? My name is

_____. I speak a little Spanish.

What's your name?

SRA. GARCÍA: My name is Carla García-

Hernandez. I speak a little English.

USTED: Nice to meet you.

SRA. GARCÍA: Yes, nice to meet you.

Using phrases found on pages 13-14, can you say the following?

✓ A greeting of your choice.

✓ My name is _____.

✓ I speak a little Spanish.

✓ Do you speak English?

✓ Speak more slowly, please.

✓ Thank you.

¿Cuál Es Su Nombre Completo?
What Is Your Complete Name?

Hispanic Names Have Four Parts

First Name	Middle Name	Father's Surname	Mother's Surname
Primer Nombre	Segundo Nombre	Apellido Paterno	Apellido Materno
Carlos	Jesús	Santana	Rodríguez
Poncho	Luis	Villa	García
Carmen	Elena	Miranda	Rivera

Start with: Señor, Señora,   or   Señorita

Use Both Names Or Only The Father's Last Name

Sr. Santana   Sr. Villa   Sra. Miranda

When A Woman Marries

She <u>keeps</u> her father's **Apellido Paterno**, and she <u>drops</u> her **Apellido Materno**
In place of her **Apellido Materno** is her husband's **Apellido Paterno**

Children Have The Apellido Paterno of
Both Father and Mother

If Carlos Santana married Carmen Miranda Rivera,
what would her name be after the marriage?
What would the baby's full name be?

José Carlos ???? ?????

Answer: *Carmen Miranda-Santana   José Carlos Santana Miranda*

16

Spanish Nouns
Can words *really* have a gender?

¡Sí! Spanish belongs to the "romance" language family. It doesn't have anything to do with love, but it has a lot to do with the Romans. In ancient times, people had the same trouble learning languages that they do today—except that there were no cassette tapes, CDs, PDAs or very many foreign language teachers. In those days, there weren't many schools for that matter! Consequently, most folks learned other languages on their own.

To help the difficult process along, words were placed into categories based upon how they sounded. It organized the material and made it easier to learn. Old world languages had categories that were often described as "masculine," "feminine," or even "neuter." From these descriptions, people began talking about words in terms of their gender. Even though the word "gender" is misleading, the tendency to group words by sound helped people learn new languages more quickly.

Because Spanish evolved from Latin, it has maintained two category divisions for thousands of years. The categories are called masculine and feminine. Even though Spanish can and will evolve, the concept of categories in *español* is not likely to change.

NOUN A person, place or thing

Here are the most important points to remember about nouns and their categories:

1. Usually, the words are grouped by how they sound, not by what they mean. There will always be a few exceptions!

2. Languages are a lot like the people who use them: They don't always follow the rules!

3. If the Spanish noun is referring to a person, the letter will often indicate the sex of that individual. For example: a doctor, who is a man, is a "*doctor*," while a woman, who is a doctor, is a "*doctora*."

4. Words in the "masculine" category usually end with the letter "O."

17

5. Words in the "feminine" category usually end with the letter "A."

6. El, la, los and las are very important words. They all mean "the."
    They are the clues you need to tell you a word's category.

El (masculine category – singular)   El niño, El muchacho
Los (masculine category – plural)   Los niños, Los muchachos
La (feminine category – singular)   La niña, La muchacha
Las (feminine category – plural)   Las niñas, Las muchachas

A Word about Adjectives

Describing things in Spanish can present many problems for English speakers. First, there is the position of the adjective in relation to the noun. In English, descriptive words go in front of the noun like "white cat,". In Spanish, the noun is the most important element, so it comes first. A white cat is *un gato blanco*. It is the opposite of our word order. It gets more complicated because there are a few basic adjectives which show size or quantity that are placed in front of the noun, just like English. These include words like large (*grande*) and small (*pequeño*), along with numbers.

Secondly, since Spanish nouns are divided into masculine and feminine categories, the adjective must match its noun by category. This means that from time to time you will need to match the letter at the end of the adjective and make it the same letter that is at the end of the noun. You must also match the adjective to the noun by number (singular or plural). This matching sound feature of Spanish is one of the main reasons it has such a musical sound. Here are several examples:

One large white cat =   Uno grande gato blanco
Three large white cats =   Tres grandes gatos blancos.

One large white house =   Una grande casa blanca
Six large white houses =   Seis grandes casas blancas

ADJECTIVE: Describes a noun

Common Adjectives—Adjetivos Comunes

These common adjectives are shown as you would find them in a Spanish dictionary. As written, use them with singular words in the masculine category, and place them behind the noun. Change the "o" at the end to an "a" to make them match up with words in the feminine category. Don't forget to add an "s" at the end for plural words.

English	Español	English	Español
Good	Bueno	Bad	Malo
Big	Grande	Small	Pequeño
Clean	Limpio	Dirty	Sucio
Hot	Caliente	Cold	Frío
Safe	Seguro	Dangerous	Peligroso
Easy	Fácil	Difficult	Difícil
Full	Lleno	Empty	Vacío
Fast	Rápido	Slow	Lento
New	Nuevo	Old	Viejo
Pretty	Bonito	Ugly	Feo
Quiet	Tranquilo	Restless	Inquieto
Tall	Alto	Short	Bajo
Well	Bien	Sick	Enfermo
Strong	Fuerte	Weak	Débil

Tips & Tidbits

Remember that learning the noun is the most important thing, not which category or gender it is! Words like "el" or "la" only mean "the." These gender markers don't give any clues to what you are trying to say. Learning the fine points of grammar can wait until you become a master of communications using Survival Spanish.

The Essentials of Spanish Verbs

There are basically three types of regular verbs in Spanish. The last two letters on the end of the verb determines how it is to be treated. Listed below are the three most common types of regular verb endings.

- ✓ **AR** – Hablar: To speak
- ✓ **ER** – Comprender: To understand
- ✓ **IR** – Escribir: To write

In Survival Spanish we focus on speaking about ourselves and talking to another person. That's the most common type of "one-on-one" communication.

When you need to say I speak, I understand, or I live, change the last two letters of the verb to an "O".

- ✓ Hablo
- ✓ Comprendo
- ✓ Escribo

When asking a question, such as do you speak, do you understand, or do you live, change the ending to an "a" or an "e." *The change in letter indicates that you are speaking to someone else.*

- ✓ Habla
- ✓ Comprende
- ✓ Escribe

To make a sentence negative, simply put "no" in front of the verb.

- ✓ No hablo
- ✓ No comprendo
- ✓ No escribo

VERB: Shows action or state of being

¡Acción!

There are so many English friendly *acción* words in the Spanish "AR" verb family. Many of them bear a strong resemblance to English verbs—most of them share a simple, regular nature. They are a very important asset in on-the-job communication. We picked a few of our favorites to get you started. Look closely at the list on the next page. On it you will recognize many comforting similarities between our languages that are practical too! Changing one letter will really expand your conversational skills.

In on-the-job conversations, people tend to use "I" and "you" to start many sentences. Of all the pronouns, these two are the most powerful and will work the best for you. So, that's where we'll start.

Here's an important difference between our languages. In English, the use of pronouns is essential because most of our verbs tend to end the same way. For example, with I speak and you speak; the verb "speak" remains the same. In English, our pronouns make all the difference. Spanish is different in this aspect. Spanish-speaking people are listening for the letters on the end of the verb. That's what indicates who or what is being talked about in Spanish. Each ending is different. The end of the Spanish verb is much more important than the beginning. The ending of the verb tells the Spanish-speaking person who or what is being discussed. In most cases when people speak Spanish, you might not hear a pronoun. It's not necessary for precise meaning. That's a big reason why Spanish might sound a little fast to you: *Pronouns which are important in English are routinely eliminated in Spanish!*

Try this: Treat the verbs in the "AR" family as you would "to speak" or "hablar." End the verb with an "o" when you're talking about yourself; "hablo" or "I speak". Change the verb ending from an "o" to an "a" for "habla" or "you speak." Use this form when you're talking to someone else.

English	Español	Guide
I need	Necesito	nay-say-SEE-toe
You need	Necesita	nay-say-SEE-ta

21

The Sweet 16 Verbs

This list of verbs contains some of the most practical one you will use on the job. Each one is in the regular –AR family, so you will find all of these to be very friendly and easy to use. Each verb is listed in its "infinitive" form, just as you would find it a dictionary. An infinitive is defined as meaning the word "to" plus the meaning of the verb.

English	Español	Guide
To ask	Preguntar	prey-goon-TAR
To bother	Molestar	mo-les-TAR
To call	Llamar	ya-MAR
To carry	Llevar	yea-VAR
To cooperate	Cooperar	co-op-air-RAR
To forget	Olvidar	ohl-v-DAR
To look at	Mirar	mear-RAHR
To need	Necesitar	nay-say-see-TAR
To observe	Observar	ob-ser-VAR
To pay	Pagar	pa-GAR
To prepare	Preparar	pray-pa-RAR
To return	Regresar	ray-grey-SAR
To study	Estudiar	es-too-d-ARE
To use	Usar	oo-SAR
To teach	Enseñar	n-sen-YAR
To work	Trabajar	tra-baa-HAR

**Note: To make a sentence negative, say no in front of the verb.
Example: I don't need. **No necesito.** You don't need **No necesita.**

Which verbs in the Sweet 16 do you use most often? List your top five:

1. _____

2. _____

3. _____

4. _____

5. _____

Now take your top six and change the AR ending to an "a" to indicate you are talking to someone else. Example: habla meaning you speak.

1. _____

2. _____

3. _____

4. _____

¡Necesito una breaka! ¿Y usted?

Irregular Verbs: The Big Five

Now that you have had the opportunity to learn about the tremendous number of verbs that follow regular patterns in Spanish, it's time to take a look at others that don't follow the rules. They are unpredictable, but they are very important. In fact, they reflect some of man's oldest concepts. That's why they tend to be irregular. These words were in use long before language rules and patterns were set. There are two verbs in Spanish that mean "to be." The others are: to have, to make and to go. Because they don't follow the rules, you will need to memorize them, but that should be easy because you will use and hear them often.

In English, the "to be" verb is I am, you are, he is, etc. The Spanish version is **ser** and **estar**. *Ser* is used to express permanent things like your nationality or profession. *Estar* is used when talking about location or conditions that change like a person's health.

	SER			ESTAR	
Yo **soy**	Nosotros **somos**		Yo **estoy**	Nosotros **estamos**	
Tú **eres**			Tú **estás**		
Él **es**	Ellos **son**		Él **está**	Ellos **están**	
Ella **es**	Ellas **son**		Ella **está**	Ellas **están**	
Usted **es**	Ustedes **son**		Usted **está**	Ustedes **están**	

The verb *"to have"* in Spanish, is *muy importante*. In English, we say that we are hot, cold, hungry, thirsty, right, wrong, or sleepy, but in Spanish those are conditions that you have. Some of those expressions mean something totally different than you expected if you get the verbs confused, so be careful!

TENER

Yo **tengo**	Nosotros **tenemos**
Tú **tienes**	
Él **tiene**	Ellos **tienen**
Ella **tiene**	Ellas **tienen**
Usted **tiene**	Ustedes **tienen**

In Spanish, the verb that means, *"to do"* also means, *"to make."* It's not unusual for one verb to have multiple meanings. There are many expressions that require the use of this verb, but you will use it most when you talk about the weather. That's a safe subject and one that everyone, the world over, discusses! **¿Qué tiempo hace?** What's the weather? **Hace frío.** (It's cold.) **Hace sol.** (It's sunny). **Hace calor.** (It's hot) **Hace viento** (It's windy.). Here's two exceptions: **Está lloviendo.** (It's raining.) and **Está nevando.** (It's snowing.)

HACER

Yo **hago**	Nosotros **hacemos**
Tú **haces**	
Él **hace**	Ellos **hacen**
Ella **hace**	Ellas **hacen**
Usted **hace**	Ustedes **hacen.**

The last of the big five is perhaps the easiest to use. It's the verb that means, *"to go"*. In Spanish, that's **ir**. It's pronounced like the English word ear. Both in English and in Spanish, we use parts of it to make the future tense, in other words, to talk about things that we are going to do. Look at the parts of *ir*. Then look back at the parts of the verb *ser*. Do you notice any similarities?

IR

Yo **voy**	Nosotros **vamos**
Tú **vas**	
Él **va**	Ellos **van**
Ella **va**	Ellas **van**
Usted **va**	Ustedes **van**

When you want to say something that you are going to do, start with I'm going or *voy*. Next, insert the word *"a"* and the basic verb that states what it is that you're going to do. Try it! It's easy. Here are some examples.

Voy a visitar a mi familia.	I am going to visit my family.
Voy a organizar el proyecto.	I am going to organize the project.
Mario va a comprar los zapatos.	Mario is going to buy the shoes.

Note: The whole concept of irregular verbs can be quite daunting. Don't let it defeat you! We have many irregular verbs in English. Every language has them. The only way to master them is to use them. Make them your own! Try writing different parts of a verb on your desk calendar. That way, it will be there in front of you every time you look down. When you see it, say it to yourself. Then, you'll have it conquered in no time.

Are you hungry? — ¿Tiene hambre?

Using the right verb at the right time is very important. The following common expressions in Spanish require the use of *tener*. These are phrases you must learn, even though the translation will feel strange to you. *Remember our English idioms often sound very strange to others.*

As a rule, *tener* is used to describe physical conditions. In English we use the verb *to be.*

TENER: To have **TENGO: I have** **TIENE: You have**

English	Español	Guide
Hot	Calor	ca-**LORE**
Hungry	Hambre	**AM**-bray
Cold	Frío.	**FREE**-oh
Ashamed	Vergüenza	ver-goo-**N**-sa
In pain.	Dolor	doe-**LORE**
Afraid of	Miedo de	me-**A**-doe day
Right	Razón	rah-**SEWN**
Thirsty	Sed	said
Sleepy	Sueño	sue-**WAYNE**-nyo
# years old	# años	# **AH**-nyos

What's the Weather? — ¿Qué tiempo hace?

No matter what the culture is a general topic for discussion is always the weather. Discussing the weather in Spanish requires a different verb from the one used in English. If you say to your host, "*Está frío,*" he or she would think that you were talking about something you had touched. In Spanish, use the verb **hacer** which means to do or to make to describe the weather. It's one of the big five irregulars.

English	Español	Guide
To be nice weather	Hace buen tiempo	AH-say boo-**WAYNE** t-**M**-po
To be hot	Hace calor	AH-say ca-**LORE**
To be cool	Hace fresco	AH-say **FRES**-co
To be sunny	Hace sol	AH-say sol
To be windy	Hace viento	AH-say v-**N**-toe
To be cold	Hace frío	AH-say **FREE**-oh
Rain	Lluvia	U-v-ah
To rain.	Llover	**YO**-ver
What's the weather?	¿Qué tiempo hace?	kay t-**M**-poe **AH**-say

Tips & Tidbits

In America we use the Fahrenheit scale for measuring the temperature. Latin Americans countries use the Celsius scale. Do you know what the difference is? Here's a simple example: 0 degrees Celsius is 32 degrees Fahrenheit.

Special Uses of Ser and Estar

The verbs *ser* and *estar* both mean the same thing in English: *to be,* but *how can two verbs mean the same thing?* It's because *ser* and *estar* are used in very different ways. Spanish sees these two verbs differently and uses them in very precise ways. Listed below are some simple guidelines on their usage:

Common Uses of Ser

A.   To express an permanent quality or characteristic

   La puerta es de madera.   The door is made of wood.

   La tienda es enorme.   The store is enormous.

   Los vendedores son importantes. Salesmen are important.

B.   To describe or identify

   Mi amigo es un cajero.   My friend is a bank teller.

   El mesero es alto.   The waiter is tall.

C.   To indicate nationality

   Pedro es mexicano.   Pedro is Mexican.

   La historia es de Argentina. The story is from Argentina.

D.   To express ownership

   Este es mi auto.   This is my car.

   Este es mi libro.   This is my book.

E.   To express time and dates

   ¿Qué hora es?   What time is it?

   Hoy es el nueve de junio.   Today is the 9th of June.

F.   With impersonal expressions.

   Es importante estudiar.   It's important to study.

   Es necesario leer.   It's necessary read.

Common Uses Of Estar

A.   To express location

   Estoy en la oficina.   I am in the office.

   Charlotte está en Carolina del Norte.   Charlotte is in North Carolina.

   El baño está en el segundo piso.   The bathroom is on the 2nd floor.

B.   To indicate someone's health

   Mi esposa está enferma.   My wife is sick.

   ¿Cómo está usted?   How are you?

C.   *Estar* is also used as a helping verb

   Estoy hablando.   I am speaking.

   Carmen está trabajando.   Carmen is working.

   Julio está regresando mañana.   Julio is returning tomorrow.

Tips & Tidbits

   Notice from the examples that *ser* is used more frequently than *estar*. Even though the usage of *ser* and *estar* seems complicated in the beginning, both verbs are used so frequently in conversation that you will become comfortable using them quickly.

The Numbers — Los Números

Number	Español	Guide
0	Cero	SAY-row
1	Uno	OO-no
2	Dos	dose
3	Tres	trays
4	Cuatro	coo-AH-trow
5	Cinco	SINK-oh
6	Seis	SAY-ees
7	Siete	see-A-tay
8	Ocho	OH-cho
9	Nueve	new-A-vay
10	Diez	d-ACE
11	Once	ON-say
12	Doce	DOSE-a
13	Trece	TRAY-say
14	Catorce	ca-TOR-say
15	Quince	KEEN-say
16	Diez y seis	d- ACE-e-SAY-ees
17	Diez y siete	d- ACE-e-see-ATE-tay
18	Diez y ocho	d- ACE-e-OH-cho
19	Diez y nueve	d- ACE-e-new-A-vay
20	Veinte	VAIN-tay
21	Veinte y uno	VAIN-tay-e-OO-no
22	Veinte y dos	VAIN-tay-e- dose
23	Veinte y tres	VAIN-tay-e-trays
24	Veinte y cuatro	VAIN-tay-e-coo-AH-trow
25	Veinte y cinco	VAIN-tay-e-SINK-oh
26	Veinte y seis	VAIN-tay-e-SAY-ees

Number	Español	Guide
27	Veinte y siete	**VAIN**-tay-e-see-**A**-tay
28	Veinte y ocho	**VAIN**-tay-e-**OH**-cho -
29	Veinte y nueve	**VAIN**-tay-e-new-**A**-vay
30	Treinta	**TRAIN**-ta
40	Cuarenta	kwah-**RAIN**-ta
50	Cincuenta	seen-**KWAIN**-ta
60	Sesenta	say-**SAIN**-ta
70	Setenta	say-**TAIN**-ta
80	Ochenta	oh-**CHAIN**-ta
90	Noventa	no-**VAIN**-ta
100	Cien	see-**IN**
200	Doscientos	dose-see-**N**-toes
300	Trescientos	tray-see-**N**-toes
400	Cuatrocientos	coo-**AH**-troh-see-**N**-toes
500	Quinientos	keen-e-**N**-toes
600	Seiscientos	**SAY**-ees-see- **N**-toes
700	Setecientos	**SAY**-tay-see- **N**-toes
800	Ochocientos	**OH**-choh- see- **N**-toes
900	Novecientos	**NO**-Vay-see- **N**-toes
1,000	Mil	meal

Tips & Tidbits

When you are speaking with a native speaker and you are talking about anything involving numbers, keep the following important information in mind:
Most people say numbers extremely fast! Don't hesitate to ask for a number to be said more slowly or to be repeated.
Review the chapter called Spanish Sounds Rápido — What Do I Do Now?

When native speakers are saying their phone numbers, you will often pair the numbers together instead of saying them as single digits.

The Days of the Week and Months of the Year
Los Días de la Semana

English	Español	Guide
Monday	lunes	LOON-ace
Tuesday	martes	MAR-tays
Wednesday	miércoles	me-AIR-co-lace
Thursday	jueves	who-WAVE-ace
Friday	viernes	v-AIR-nace
Saturday	sábado	SAH-ba-doe
Sunday	domingo	doe-MING-go

When expressing a date in Spanish, give the number of the day first. Follow the day with the month. Use this format: El (date) de (month).

LOS MESES DEL AÑO

English	Español	Guide
January	enero	n-NAY-row
February	febrero	fay-BRAY-row
March	marzo	MAR-so
April	abril	ah-BRILL
May	mayo	MY-oh
June	junio	WHO-knee-oh
July	julio	WHO-lee-oh
August	agosto	ah-GOSE-toe
September	septiembre	sep-tee-EM-bray
October	octubre	oc-TOO-bray
November	noviembre	no-v-EM-bray
December	diciembre	d-see-EM-bray

Your appointment is (day of the week) el (number) de (month).
Su cita es lunes, el 11 de octubre.

Practicing Numbers & Dates

Practice these important items by using numbers, days of the week, and months of the year:

- ✓ Your social security number

- ✓ Your driver's license number

- ✓ The numbers in your address

- ✓ Your zip code

- ✓ Your phone number

- ✓ Your birth date

- ✓ Your children's birth dates

- ✓ The dates of holidays

- ✓ License tags of the cars in front of you, when you are stopped in traffic.

Combine the Spanish alphabet with this exercise.

- ✓ Phone numbers you see on billboards

- ✓ Numbers found on street signs

- ✓ Phone numbers when you dial them at work or at home

- ✓ The appointments on your personal calendar

- ✓ Your wedding anniversary

- ✓ The dates of all your Spanish classes or practice sessions

What Time Is It? — ¿Qué Hora Es?

The concept of time is something that varies from culture to culture. Many countries put less emphasis on being on time for certain things than Americans do. In Latino culture one lives for the present. It can be especially true in one's personal life; however, on the job everyone knows the value of *puntualidad. ¡Es muy importante!*

Learning to tell time is another good way to put your numbers in Spanish to good use *¿Qué hora es?* means *what time is it?*

It's one o'clock.	Es la una.
It's two o'clock.	Son las dos.
It's 3:30.	Son las tres y media.
It's 5:45.	Son las seis menos quince.

Use the phrases *de la mañana* to indicate morning and *de la tarde* to indicate afternoon. Also midnight is *medianoche.* Noon is *mediodía.*

To find out at what time something takes place ask: *¿A qué hora…?*

¿A qué hora es la reunión?	What time is the meeting?
¿A qué hora termina?	What time do you finish?

Spanish speakers sometimes use the 24-hour clock for departures and arrivals of trains and flights, etc.

12:05	las doce cero cinco
17.52	las diez y siete cincuenta y dos
23.10	las veinte y tres diez
07.15	las siete quince

Para Practicar

1. Using the word for meeting *"la reunion,"* say that your meeting takes place on the hour throughout your workday. *La reunión es a las ocho.*

Scheduling an Appointment

When you need to schedule an appointment, this form will come in very handy for you. In *español* an appointment is called a *cita* (SEE-ta). List the name of the individual that the appointment is with first. Then circle the day of the week and add the number for the day. Finally, circle the month and add the time. The phrase at the bottom of this form simply asks the individual to arrive ten minutes early for the appointment.

Usted tiene una cita importante con _____.

La cita es   lunes   el _____ de   enero   a las _____.

                 martes   febrero

                 miércoles   marzo

                 jueves   abril

                 viernes   mayo

                                               junio

                                               julio

                                               agosto

                                               septiembre

                                               octubre

                                               noviembre

                                               diciembre

**Favor de llegar 10 minutos antes del tiempo de su cita. ¡Gracias!

Please arrive 10 minutes before the time of your appointment. Thank you.

The Questions Everyone Should Know

English	Español	Guide
Who?	¿Quién?	key-N
What?	¿Qué?	kay
Which?	¿Cuál?	coo-ALL
When?	¿Cuándo?	KWAN-doe
Where?	¿Dónde?	DON-day
Why?	¿Por qué?	pour KAY
How?	¿Cómo?	CO-mo
What's happening?	¿Qué pasa?	kay PA-sa
How much?	¿Cuánto?	KWAN-toe
How many?	¿Cuántos?	KWAN-toes

When you ask a question in Spanish, it will take on the same form as a question does in English. Start with the question word that asks the information you need. Follow the question word with a verb, and give your voice an upward inflection.

In Spanish you can also make a question by ending your sentence with ¿no? Here's an example: *Cancún está en México, ¿no?* When you end a sentence with "no" like this, it takes on the meaning of "isn't it."

The Most Common Questions

How are you?	¿Cómo está?
How much does it cost?	¿Cuánto cuesta?
Where are you from?	¿De dónde es?

To make the Spanish upside down question mark or the upside down exclamation mark refer, to the chapter called "Typing in Spanish on Your Computer."

Getting the Información

Listed below are common phrases that are used to fill out almost any questionnaire. It seems like most forms always ask for much of the same information in almost the same order. By learning a few simple phrases, you can use this format to your advantage.

There are so many times when we need to ask for very basic information. Most of these questions begin with the words "*what is your.*" When you are asking this type of question, remember that it's not always necessary to make a complete sentence to have good communication. The information you are asking for is much more important than the phrase "what is your"? As long as you remember to make what you say *sound* like a question by giving your voice an *upward* inflection, people will interpret what you've said *as* a question.

Use the form on the following page. It asks for very basic information. To help you practice, work with a partner. Make up new information about yourself and complete the form. At each practice session one of you will ask the questions and the other will give the answers to fill in the information requested. This is a great practice exercise, because when you think about it, most of the time the questions you ask will be the same, but the answers you get will always be different!

| **What is your** | | **¿Cuál es su?** |
| | | coo-**ALL** es sue |

English	Español	Guide
Full name	Nombre completo	NOM-bray com-**PLAY**-toe
First name	Primer nombre	pre-**MARE** NOM-bray
Middle name	Segundo nombre	say-**GOON**-doe NOM-bray
Last name (surname)	Apellido	ah-pay-**YE**-doe
Paternal surname	Apellido paterno	ah-pay-**YE**-doe pa-**TER**-no

37

English	Español	Guide
Maternal surname	Apellido materno	ah-pay-YE-doe ma-TER-no
Address	Dirección	d-wreck-see-ON
Apartment number	Número de apartamento	NEW-may-row day ah-par-ta-MEN-toe
Age	Edad	a-DAD
Date of birth	Fecha de nacimiento	FAY-cha day na-see-me-N-toe
Nationality	Nacionalidad	na-see-on-nal-e-DAD
Place of birth	Lugar de nacimiento	loo-GAR day na-see-me-N-toe
Place of employment	Lugar de empleo	loo-GAR day m-PLAY-oh
Occupation	Ocupación	oh-coo-pa-see-ON
Home telephone number	Número de teléfono de su casa	NEW-may-row day tay-LAY-fo-no day sue CA-sa
Work telephone number	Número de teléfono de su empleo	NEW-may-row day tay-LAY-fo-no day sue m-PLAY-oh
Marital status	Estado civil	es-TA-doe see-VEAL
Married	Casado (a)	ca-SA-doe
Single	Soltero (a)	soul-TAY-row
Divorced	Divorciado (a)	d-vor-see-AH-doe
Widow	Viudo (a)	v-OO-doe
Separated	Separado (a)	sep-pa-RAH-doe
Driver's license number	Número de licencia	NEW-may-row day lee-SEN-see-ah
Social security number	Número de seguro social	NEW-may-row day say-GOO-row sew-see-AL

Información Básica
Imprima por favor

Fecha: _____
                              Mes   Día   Año

Sr.
Sra.
Srta. _____
      Primer Nombre   Segundo Nombre   Apellido Paterno   Apellido Materno (Esposo)

Dirección: _____
                                     Calle

_____
Ciudad   **Estado**   **Zona postal**

Teléfono: Casa _____   **Empleo** _____

          Cel _____   **Fax** _____

Correo electrónico _____

Número de seguro social: _____-_____-_____   **Fecha de nacimiento** _____
                                                            Mes   Día   Año

Número de la licencia: _____

Ocupación: _____

Lugar de empleo _____

Estado civil: ☐ Casado (a)   ☐ Divorciado (a)   ☐ Viudo (a)
                    ☐ Soltero (a)   ☐ Separado (a)

Nombre de esposo: _____
      Primer Nombre   Segundo Nombre   Apellido Paterno   Apellido Materno

Nombre de esposa: _____
      Primer Nombre   Segundo Nombre   Apellido Paterno Apellido Materno/Esposo

En caso de emergencia: _____ **Teléfono:** _____

Firma: _____ **Fecha:** _____

See back of book for English translation of the basic information form.

The Family — La Familia

Putting our families first is something all Americans have in common. It is especially true for Latinos. For them, family values are extremely important. No sacrifice is too great if it helps the family. Children are considered to be precious gifts. Wives, mothers, and grandmothers are highly respected. Remember, that the maternal side of the family is so important that traditionally Hispanics carry their mother's surname or *materno apellido* as a part of their complete name. If you have forgotten the four important parts of a Latino's name, please review the chapter called *"Cuál es su nombre completo."*

You are certainly going to hear about members of the family from your Hispanic customers. It's something all of us like to talk about!

English	Español	Guide
Aunt	Tía	T-ah
Uncle	Tío	T-oh
Brother	Hermano	air-MAN-oh
Sister	Hermana	air-MAN-ah
Brother-in-law	Cuñado	coon-YA-doe
Sister-in-law	Cuñada	coon-YA-da
Child	Niño *(m)*	KNEE-nyo
	Niña *(f)*	KNEE-nya
Cousin	Primo *(m)*	PRE-mo
	Prima *(f)*	PRE-ma
Daughter	Hija	E-ha
Son	Hijo	E-ho

English	Español	Guide
Daughter-in-law	Nuera	new-**AIR**-rah
Son-in-law	Yerno	**YAIR**-no
Father	Padre	**PA**-dray
Mother	Madre	**MA**-**dray**
Father-in-law	Suegro	soo-**A**-grow
Mother-in-law	Suegra	soo-**A**-gra
Niece	Sobrina	so-**BREE**-na
Nephew	Sobrino	so-**BREE**-no
Step father	Padrastro	pa-**DRAS**-tro
Step mother	Madrastra	ma-**DRAS**-tra
Step son	Hijastro	e-**HAS**-tro
Step daughter	Hijastra	e-**HAS**-tra
Granddaughter	Nieta	knee-**A**-ta
Grandson	Nieto	knee-**A**-toe
Grandfather	Abuelo	ah-boo-**A**-low
Grandmother	Abuela	ah-boo-**A**-la
Husband	Esposo	**es-POE-so**
Wife	Esposa	es-**POE**-sa

Para Practicar

Using the verb tener (to have), tell your practice partner how many relatives you have in your family. Start like this: Tengo or I have. Follow that with the number and the member of the family that you are talking about. Tener is covered in the chapter on the five most important irregular verbs in Spanish called the "Big Five" Even though tener isn't a regular verb, it's very practical. You will use it mucho. **Example**: Tengo una hermana. I have one sister.

Employee Benefits and Human Resources
Beneficios y Recoursos Humanos

As you might expect, employment practices are very different in Latin America than they are in the US. The concept of deductions for taxes and insurance might be completely new for a first generation Hispanic employee. It's very rare for a worker, especially an hourly wage earner, to receive benefits such as health insurance or paid vacations in Latin America. Your benefit package may be different in both concept and practice from what this employee has experienced before — explain it to him very slowly — especially if payroll deductions are involved. No one likes surprises on pay day.

For an important meeting like this one where you want to get started out on the right foot, it's important to be well-prepared. Make a check list of all the vocabulary you are likely to use. Practice pronouncing these words and phrases before the meeting takes place. Make as many notes as you want, and remember to go at your own speed. Take all the time you need! You will be able to communicate much more effectively if you aren't nervous. Your new employee will certainly appreciate your effort. Allow time and make the opportunity for your new hire to ask questions. The ability to express opinions and discuss options is highly valued in Latin American culture. Never close this important door to communications! This meeting marks the beginning of a valuable relationship you are building with this employee. After your conference is over, review your notes again. Mark the areas where you felt comfortable and did well. Highlight the areas where you feel you need more work or additional practice. Each time you need to explain benefits to a Spanish-speaking employee, you'll get better and better.

English	Español	Guide
Benefits	Beneficios	ben-nay-**FEE**-see-ohs
Check	Cheque	**CHEC**-kay
Disability	Incapacidad	n-ka-pah-see-**DAD**
Holidays	Días festivos	**DEE**-ahs fes-**T**-vos
Medical insurance	Seguro médico	say-**GOO**-row **MAY**-d-co
Overtime	Sobre tiempo	so-bray-t-**M**-po
Paid vacations	Vacaciones pagadas	va-ca-see-**ON**-ace pa-**GA**-das
Paycheck	Paga	**PAH**-ga
Permanent residence card	Tarjeta de residencia	tar-**HEY**-ta day ray-see-**DEN**-c-a
Retirement	Retiro	ray-**TEE**-row
	Jubilación	who-bee-la-see-**ON**
Severance pay	Indemnización por despedida	in-dem-knee-za-see-**ON** pour days-pay-**DEE**-dah
Sick leave	Días pagados por enfermedad	**DEE**-ahs pah-**GA**-dos pour in-fer-may-**DAD**
Social security	Seguro social	say-**GOO**-row so-see-**AL**
Tax deductions	Deducciones de impuestos	day-duck-sc-**ON**-aces day em-poo-**ES**-toes
Taxes	Impuestos	em-poo-**ES**-toes
Unemployment insurance	Seguro de desempleo	say-**GOO**-row day des-em-**PLAY**-oh
Worker's compensation	Compensación de obrero	com-pen-za-see-**ON** day o-**BRAY**-row

Employee Motivation
Motivación de Empleados

It doesn't matter what language we speak, all of us need a daily dose of encouragement. Words that motivate are extremely powerful and positive. One of the hallmarks of a good manager is having a positive attitude and sharing that energy in the workplace. In a Latin American company it is customary for supervisors to speak with each member of the team at the start of the work day. A smile, a warm welcome and a few words of motivation set a great tone for everyone's day. The few minutes you spend helps your employees feel like they are an important part of the team. You may find that this part of your day is extremely rewarding. One thing is certain: all of your employees will appreciate your efforts. A big smile will go a long way when you use these phrases.

English	Español	Guide
It's…!	¡Es…!	es
Excellent	Excelente	x-see-**LEN**-tay
Fantastic	Fantástico	fan-**TAS**-t-co
Good	Bueno	boo-**WAY**-no
Extraordinary	Extraordinario	x-tra-or-d-**NAR**-ree-oh
Magnificent	Magnífico	mag-**KNEE**-fee-co
What good work!	¡Qué buen trabajo!	kay boo-**WAYNE** tra-**BAA**-ho
Very good!	¡Muy bien!	mooy b-**N**
You're very important!	¡Usted es muy importante!	oo-**STED** es mooy m-por-**TAN**-tay
You're very professional.	¡Usted es muy profesional!	oo-**STED** es mooy pro-fes-see-on-**NAL**

English	Español	Guide
You learn quickly.	Aprende rápido.	ah-PREN-day RAH-p-doe
I respect you.	Le respeto.	lay race-PAY-toe
You are very valuable.	¡Usted es valioso!	oo-STED es val-ee-OH-so
There is…	Hay…	eye
Advancement	Ascenso	ahs-SEN-so
Opportunity	Oportunidad	oh-por-too-knee-DAD
Great potential	Gran potencial	gran po-ten-see-AL
Obvious progress	Progreso obvio	pro-GRES-oh OB-v-oh
Positive Feedback	Reacción positiva	ray-ax-see-ON po-see-T-va
Realistic goals	Metas posibles	MAY-tas po-SEE-blays

Be sincere
on time
Don't exaggerate
Only when needed *Don't give and take back.*

Tips & Tidbits

In a Latin American company the boss or "*el jefe*" (HEF-a) takes a very personal interest in his or her employees. A boss who is female is called "*la jefa*" (HEF-ah). This attitude is called "*personalismo*," and it's extremely important in Latin American business settings. The relationship between a Hispanic manager and his employees is very strong. A good manager not only knows the names of all his employees; he also knows the names of their children and wives. Often a Hispanic manager will become so involved in the personal lives of his staff that they feel comfortable asking his advice on very personal matters. To help an employee, *el jefe* will bend the rules if necessary and makes a point of "taking care of his own," even if doing so isn't the most cost-effective decision.

PATERNALISTIC

Employee Evaluations
Evaluación de Empleados

Employee performance appraisals usually occur at regular intervals and are important for both the employee and the employer. Evaluating an employee's performance on the job helps any business function with better efficiency. The employee should know both strengths in addition to areas of performance that need improvement. Everyone appreciates knowing where they stand!

When evaluating a Latin American employee, keep these important tips in mind:

1. Make sure to get up from your desk. Then, walk around it to greet your employee and shake hands. Indicate where you wish them to sit.

2. If your office has a seating area away from your desk, take advantage of it. By sitting in a chair beside your employee, you will put him at ease. This removes the desk as an obstacle between you.

3. Don't "cut to the chase" and begin your evaluation immediately. Have some conversation first. Ask about your employee's family. A little informal conversation will put both of you more at ease and help you build a better relationship

4. After you have completed your evaluation, ask for your employee's opinion. Your Hispanic employee will welcome the opportunity to share ideas with you openly.

After you study this section of vocabulary, review your company's evaluation form. What words from this chapter could help you? Start a form in Spanish to help you prepare for these important conferences. You'll feel better knowing you are prepared!

English	Español	Guide
The company needs to evaluate	La compañía necesita evaluar	la com-pa-**KNEE**-ah nay-say-**SEE**-ta a-val-oo-**ARE**
Goals	Metas	**MAY**-tas
Objectives	Objetivos	ob-hey-**T**-vos
Strengths	Puntos fuertes	**POON**-toes foo-**AIR**-tays
Weaknesses	Debilidades	day-b-lee-**DAD**-aces
Ability	Habilidad	ah-b-lee-**DAD**
Communication	Comunicación	co-moo-knee-ca-se-**ON**
Control	Control	con-**TROL**
Knowledge	Conocimiento	co-no-see-me-**N**-toe
Language	Lenguaje	len-goo-**AH**-hey
Potential	Potencial	po-ten-see-**AL**
Talent	Talento	ta-**LEN**-toe
The company needs to improve	La compañía necesita mejorar	la com-pa-**KNEE**-ah nay-say-**SEE**-ta may-hor-**RARE**
Production	Producción	pro-duke-see-**ON**
Quality	Calidad	ca-lee-**DAD**
Service	Servicio	ser-**V**-see-oh
Operation	Operación	oh-pear-rah-see-**ON**

Don't let your desk become a barrier for good communications. Get up and sit beside your employee. If that's not possible because of the furniture arrangement in your office, move your chair beside your desk or in front of it.

Utilities — Utilidades

Working for a utility company puts you on the front lines of customer service. You are there to help with a variety of crucial services including electricity, gas, and water. It doesn't matter if your company is private or a part of city-county government services—everyone depends on you—no matter what language they speak. If you handle telephone communication or face-to-face customer service, the following phrases will help you explain everything from account numbers to meter reading.

English	Español	Guide
Account number	Número de cuenta	NEW-may-row day QUAIN-ta
Air Conditioning	Aire acondicionado	eye-RAY ah-con-d-c-oh-NA-doe
Contract	Contracto	con-TRAH-toe
Date	Fecha	FAY-cha
Deposit	Depósito	day-PO-see-toe
Furnace	Horno	OR-no
Gas	Gas	gas
Guarantor	Garante	gah-RAN-tay
Mailing Address	Dirección de correo	dee-wreck-see-ON day co-RAY-oh
Payment	Pago	PA-go
Payment plan	Plan de pagos	plan day PA-gos
Seller	Vendedor	ven-day-DOOR
Service	Servicio	ser-V-see-oh
At what time	¿A qué hora?	ah kay HOR-ah

English	Español	Guide
It costs $___ to transfer your service.	Cuesta $___ transferir su servicio.	coo-A-sta $___ transfer-REAR sue ser-V-see-oh
It costs $_____ to reconnect your service.	Cuesta $_____ reconectarse su servicio.	coo-A-sta $_____ ray-co-nec-TAR-say sue ser-V- see-oh
Please fill out this form.	Favor de llenar esta forma.	fa-VOR day yea-NAR ES-ta FOR-ma
I need the serial number of the meter.	Necesito el número de serie del contador.	nay-say-SEE-toe el NEW-may-row day SER-ree-a del con-ta-DOOR
The serial number has ____ digits.	El número de serie tiene _____ números.	el NEW-may-row day SER-ree-a t-N-a ____ NEW-may-rows
You need to read the meter.	Necesita leer el contador.	nay-say-SEE-toe l ay-AIR el con-ta-DOOR
Where is the house located?	¿Dónde está la casa ubicado? a	DON-day es-TA la CA-sa oo-b-CA-doe
Please sign your name.	Favor de firmar su nombre.	fa-VOR day fear-MAR sue NOM-bray
Who is paying the bill?	¿Quién paga la cuenta?	key-N PA-ga la coo-AIN-ta

One of the most challenging parts of your job will be speaking Spanish to customers on the telephone. To help you with this important part of your job, make a quick reference guide of the phrases you need most often, and keep it under the telephone. It will always be there when you need it!

Para Practicar

1. A Spanish-speaking customer calls ask for the account number.

   _____

2. Tell your customer that you need the number on the meter.

   _____

3. Your customer's service has been disconnected. Tell the customer how much the fee is for reinstatement.

   _____

4. Your customer is moving. How much is the fee is for service transfer.

   _____

5. What is the amount of your company's deposit?

   _____

6. Ask your customer to fill out your application for service.

   _____

7. Using the numbers and days of the week, when is your office open?

   _____

8. What is the telephone number to your office?

   _____

9. What is your after-hours customer service number?

   _____

10. Ask what time is most convenient for your technician to connect the service.

    _____

11. Tell your customer how many digits your serial numbers contain.

    _____

12. Ask for the complete name of the person who is responsible for the bill.

    _____

Do You Need to Finance?
¿Necesita financiar?

Establishing credit and accounts for basic services like electricity, gas, telephone, and other utilities can be extremely daunting to your customers with limited English proficiency. Every company is different and it's impossible to know what to expect in every situation. There are so many forms to fill out and deposits to put up in order to get service established. It's easy to become overwhelmed.

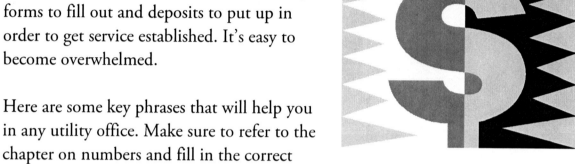

Here are some key phrases that will help you in any utility office. Make sure to refer to the chapter on numbers and fill in the correct amounts for your company charges for deposits, late fees and credit application processing. Practice these numbers often. Having these important numbers handy when you need them will take lots of pressure off your shoulders!

English	Español	Guide
Do you need financing?	¿Necesita financiar?	nay-say-SEE-ta fee-nan-see-ARE
Do you have a cost estimate from the contractor?	¿Tiene una estimación de gastos del contratista?	t-N-a OO-na s-t-ma-c-ON del con-tra-T-sta?
Please wait a moment.	Favor de esperar un momento.	fa-VOR day es-pear-RAR oon mo-MEN-toe
I need to make a copy.	Necesito hacer una copia.	nay-say-SEE-toe ah-SER OO-na CO-p-ah

English	Español	Guide
There is a fee for processing your credit application.	Hay una cuota de servicio para procesar su solicitud de crédito.	ay OO-na coo-OH-ta day ser-V-see-oh PA-rah pro-say-SAR sue so-lee-see-TOOD dayCRAY-dee-toe
It is not reimbursable.	No es reembolsable.	no es ray-m-bowl-SA-blay.
If you have a gas water heater your finance rate is _____%.	Si tiene un calentador de agua que funciona con gas, su por ciento de financiación es _____ por ciento.	see tee-N-a oon ka-lent-ta-DOOR day ah-goo-ah kay foon-see-OH-na con gas sue pour see-N-toe day fee-nan-c-ah-see-ON es _____ pour see-N-toe.
Please fill out the credit application.	Favor de llenar la solicitud de crédito.	fa-VOR day yea-NAR la so-lee-see-TOOD day CRAY-d-toe
We can finance up to 5 years.	Podemos financiar hasta cinco años.	po-DAY-mos fee-nan-see-ARE AH-sta SINK-co AN-yos
Your payments will be _#_ per month.	Su pago es _#_ mensualmente.	sue pago es _#_ men-sue-al-MEN-tay
Here is your contract.	Aquí está su contrato.	ah-KEY es-TA sue con-TRA-toe
This is your total finance charge.	Esta es su cuenta completa de finanzas.	ES-ta es sue coo-WAYN-ta com-PLAY-ta day fee-NAN-sas

English	Español	Guide
I need your complete signature here.	Favor de firmar su nombre completo aquí.	fa-**VOR** day fear-**MAR** sue nom-**BRAY** com-**PLAY**-toe ah-**KEY**
This legal document is a UCC-1.	Este documento legal es un UCC-1.	**ES**-tay doe-coo-**MEN**-toe lay-**GAL** es un oo-say-say-uno.
If you finance or sell your home, this loan will need to be paid before the property can legally change owners.	Si necesita financiar o vender su casa, debe que pagar este préstamo primero o la propiedad no puede cambiar propietarios.	see nay-say-**SEE**-ta fee-nan-see-**ARE** oh ven-**DARE** sue **CA**-sa day-bay kay pa-**GAR** **ES**-tay **PRESS**-ta-mo pre-**MARE**-row oh la pro-p-a-**DAD** no poo-**A**-day cam-b-**ARE** pro-p-a-**TAR**-ree-ohs
I will call you as soon as I receive your application back from the credit department.	Voy a llamar por teléfono cuando recibo su solicitud del departamento de crédito.	voy ah ya-**MAR** pour tay-**LAY**-fono **KWAN**-doe ray-**SEE**-bo sue so-lee-see-**TOOD** del day-par-ta-**MENTO** day **CRAY**-d-to

Uniform commercial code form

Tips & Tidbits
1. Rather than using personal checks or credit cards, many Latinos prefer paying their bills *en efectivo"* or in cash.
2. For many Latino families owning a home rather than renting is seen as being good for the family's well-being. Recent studies estimate that 50% of Latino net worth is found in home ownership.

Para Practicar

Señor Juan Gilberto Perez Peña wants to have electricity connected to his apartment. He also wants to purchase a new gas hot water heater. Find out his address, the date he needs his service connected, and tell him your company requires a $25 non-refundable fee to process his credit application. You will also need to discuss finance charges for the purchase of the appliance. Good luck!

1. Complete name

    _____

2. Date of service

    _____

3. New address

    _____

4. Previous address

    _____

5. Fee _____

6. Ask for Mr. Perez Peña's signature on the application _____

    _____

7. Ask for identification. _____

8. Tell Sr. Perez Peña that you will call him when his credit application is approved.

    _____

In the Hospital Business Office

There's nothing more important in the hospital than great patient care—and accurate paperwork. The financial world of healthcare makes the hospital world go around! The paperwork can be extremely complicated and patients are under extreme amounts of pressure. So are you. This situation is certainly a challenge under the best of circumstances. Add the language barrier and now you've really got something! As you begin to examine the phrases you need to learn in Spanish, also think about greetings and phrases that will make your patient comfortable. Look for appropriate phrases in the "One for the Road" chapter at the end of your book. Here is a list of words and phrases that will help get it straight and keep it all together.

English	Español	Guide
Account number	Número de cuenta	NEW-may-row day coo-AINT-ta
Billing/invoice	Factura	fac-TOO-rah
Business office	Oficina de negocios	oh-fee-SEEN-na day nay-GO-see-ohs
Cash	En efectivo	n a-fec-T-vo
Checks	Cheques	CHAY-kays
Claimant	Reclamante *SOLICITANTE*	ray-cla-MAHN-tay
Claims	Reclamación	ray-cla-ma-see-ON
Collection	Colección	co-leck-see-ON
Computer	Computadora	com-poo-ta-DOOR-ah
Contact	Contacto	con-TACK-toe
Co-payment	Pago compartido	PA-go com-par-T-do

55

English	Español	Guide
Copy	Copia	CO-p-ah
Coverage	Cobertura	co-bear-TWO-rah
Credit card	Tarjeta de crédito	tar-HEY-ta day CRAY-d-toe
Date of service	Fecha de servicio	FAY-cha day ser-V-see-oh
Department	Departamento	day-par-ta-MEN-toe
Doctor's name	Nombre de doctor	NOM-bray day doc-TOR
Email	Correo electrónico	co-RAY-oh a-lec-TRON-knee-co
Expiration date	Fecha de vencimiento	FAY-cha de ven-c-me-N-toe
Explanation of benefits	Explicación de beneficios	x-plea-ca-see-ON day bay-nay-FEE-see-ohs
Fax	Facsímile	fac-SEE-me-lay
Insurance card	Tarjeta de seguro médico	tar-HEY-ta day say-GOO-row MAY-dee-co
Insurance – primary	Seguro médico primario	say-GOO-row MAY-d-co pre-MAR-ree-oh
Insurance – secondary	Seguro médico segundario	say-GOO-row MAY-d-co say-goon-DAR-ree-oh
Itemized bill	Factura en detalle	fac-TOO-rah en day-TA-yea
Liability	Responsabilidad	rays-pon-sa-b-lee-DAD
Mail (n)	Correo	co-RAY-oh
Money order	Giro postal	HE-row pos-TAL

56

English	Español	Guide
Monthly payment	Pagos mensual	**PA**-gos men-sue-**AL**
Orthopedic	Ortopédico	or-toe-**PAY**-d-co
Payment	Pago	**PA**-go
Payment arrangements	Plan de pago	plan day **PA**-go
Refunds	Reembolso	ray-m-**BOWL**-so
Request	Solicitud	so-lee-see-**TOOD**
Return	Regresar *(v)*	ray-grey-**SAR**
Same-day	Mismo día	**MEES**-mo D-ah
Social security number	Número de seguro social	**NEW**-may-row day say-**GOO**-row so-see-**AL**
Supervisor	Supervisor *(a)*	sue-pear-v-**SOAR**
Surgery	Cirugía	sear-roo-**HE**-ah

SEGURO = SAFE = FOR SURE = INSURANCE

Tips & Tidbits

The Spanish word *"seguro"* is used in many important phrases. Even though this word actually means "insurance," it is also a part of the translation of "Social Security." In Spanish that's *"seguro social"* (say-**GOO**-row so-see-**AL**). This phrase is one of the many in our two languages that don't translate identically. It is more of a "concept" translation than a literal one. Most Latin American countries don't have "social security" or other public assistance programs, so our Social Security is viewed as being a sort of "social insurance." Review the following phrases where the word *"seguro"* is used.

1. Medical insurance   Seguro medico
2. Dental insurance   Seguro dental
3. Disability insurance   Seguro de incapacidad
4. Social security   Seguro social

In The Bank — En El Banco

When working as a bank teller (*cajero* or *cajera*), or in any type of customer service position, efficiency and accuracy are both critical to your success with customers. Begin each transaction with kindness, courtesy, and *mucha paciencia*

 because your Latino customers could be nervous about speaking English or about presenting identification. Never make the assumption that your Spanish-speaking customer isn't a resident of your local community or that he doesn't have an account with your bank. That could be a very embarrassing mistake!

Work to build strong relationships — using courtesy titles like *señor, señora* or *señorita* are a good way to welcome people and show respect. There's nothing more important than developing a communications strategy to assist your new customers. Happy, well-treated people become loyal customers and provide your banking institution with many new referrals, too.

Here are some important tips for good communication in the bank:

1. Do **not** speak loudly if you aren't understood the first time! You can disrupt the atmosphere of the whole customer service area. Your customers aren't accustomed to hearing you yell!

2. When you speak English, go slowly and carefully. Never shorten words like identification to ID or photograph to photo. These are abbreviations or slang, which are very hard to learn.

3. Remember that when you are speaking English your customer is translating what you are saying back into their own language, coming up with an answer, and then translating that answer back into English. This process takes some time. *Impatience on your part will make this process take longer because you may make your customer anxious or forgetful.*

4. Use body language or write notes to help you make yourself understood, especially where numbers are concerned.

5. **Never** laugh at a person's attempt to speak English. After all, English is one of the world's hardest languages, and if you laugh, all communication will stop cold!

6. **Don't rush through the transaction!** Hispanic customers want to establish a rapport with you. That's usually more important than moving quickly through the line. Take your time

English	Español	Guide
May I help you?	¿Puedo ayudarle?	pooh-A-doe eye-you-DAR-lay
Do you need	Necesita	nay-say-SEE-ta
To cash your check	Cobrar su cheque	co-BRAR sue CHECK-kay
To make a deposit	Hacer un depósito	ah-SER oon day-PO-see-toe
To open a checking account	Abrir una cuenta corriente	ah-BRIER OO-na coo-WAYNE-ta core-ree-N-tay
To apply for a personal loan	Solicitar un préstamo personal	so-lee-see-TAR oon PRAY-sta-mo pear-so-NAL
To apply for a check card	Solicitar una tarjeta de débito	so-lee-see-TAR OO-na tar-HEY-ta day DAY-b-toe
To deposit into savings	Depositar en su cuenta de ahorros	day-po-see-TAR en sue coo-WAYNE-ta day ah-OAR-rows
Deposit slip	Boleta de depósito	OO-na bow-LAY-ta day day-PO-see-toe
How much?	¿Cuánto?	coo-AHN-toe
I need two forms of identification.	Necesito dos formas de identificación.	nay-say-SEE-toe dose FOR-mas day e-den-t-fee-ca-c-ON
I need your identification with a photograph.	Necesito su identificación con una fotografía.	nay-say-SEE-toe sue e-den-t-fee-ca-c-ON con OO-na foe-toe-gra-FEE-ah
You need to endorse your check here.	Necesita endorsar su cheque aquí.	nay-say-SEE-ta en-door-SAR sue CHECK-kay ah-KEY
Please sign here.	Favor de firmar aquí.	fa-VOR day fear-MAR ah-KEY

Other Banking Processes

English	Español	Guide
Do you need…?	¿Necesita…?	nay-say-**SEE**-ta
Auto loan	Préstamo para un auto	oon **PREY**-sta-mo **PA**-rah oon **OW**-toe
Cash	En efectivo	n eh-fec-**T**-vo
CD	Certificado de depósito	cer-t-fee-**CA**-doe day day-**PO**-see-toe
Direct deposit	Depósito directo	day-**PO**-see-toe dee-**WRECK**-toe
Home equity line of credit	Línea de crédito hipotecario	**LEE**-nay-ah day **CRAY**-d-toe e-po-teh-**CA**-ree-ah
Home loan	Préstamo para una casa	oon **PREY**-sta-mo **PA**-rah **OO**-na **CA**-sa
Internet services	Servicios de Internet	ser-**V**-see-ohs day een-ter-**NET**
IRA	Cuenta de retiro individual	coo-**WAYNE**-ta day ray-**TEA**-row een-d-v-do-**AL**
Money order	Giro postal	**HE**-row pos-**TAL**
Money transfer	Transferencia de dinero	trans-feh-**WREN**-c-ah day dee-**NAIR**-row
Refinance	Refinanciar	reh-fee-nan-see-**ARE**
Student loan	Préstamo para educación	**PREY**-sta-mo **PA**-rah eh-do-ca-see-**ON**
To make a withdrawal	Hacer un retiro	ah-**SER** oon ray-**T**-row
To use the automatic teller	Usar el cajero automático	oo-**SAR** el ca-**HAIR**-row ow-toe-**MA**-t-co
To verify your balance	Verificar su saldo	ver-ree-fee-**CAR** sue **SAL**-doe

Para Practicar

1. Señor Juan Antonio Marcos Ríos would like to cash his check. Verify his identification. Then tell him where he should endorse it.

   2 FORMAS DE IDENTIDAD
   ENDORSE ~~AL PIE~~ SU CHEQUE AQUÍ
   _____

2. Señorita Lillian Baker-Colón needs to apply for a check card and to open a savings account.

   TARJETA DE BANCO
   CUENTA DE AHORROS
   _____

3. Señor Emilio Díaz Cruz wants to open a checking account. Ask for the following information:

   a. Complete name _____

   b. Address _____

   c. Home telephone number _____

   d. Date of birth _____

   e. Social security number _____

4. Señora Hernandez-Saavedra would like to sign-up for on-line banking services.

   SERVICIO de BANCO por INTERNET
   _____

Even though you might have a line out the door, take extra care of your clients that don't speak English as their first language. To them, building a relationship with you can be more important than the transaction itself!

Collection — Colección

Collecting past due accounts are at best a difficult job. Add the fact that most collections are done over the phone and you have an additional barrier to good communication. There's no body language to help you and you can't write down the numbers you need and show them to your client. Make a script before you start so you will be prepared with the vocabulary you need. Always keep your cool, be polite, and keep your Spanish phrases close at hand. It's also a good idea to practice what you are going to say before you call, and to anticipate what you might hear from the other end of the phone. Use the following phrases and bits of vocabulary and write your own script to help you in these situations.

English	Español	Guide
Accounts payable	Cuenta a pagar	coo-WAYNE-ta ah pa-GAR
Accounts receivable	Cuenta a cobrar	coo-WAYNE-ta ah co-BRAR
Additional charge	Recargo adicional	ray-CAR-go ah-d-see-oh-NAL
Amount	Suma	SUE-ma
Amount due	Cantidad debido	can-t-DAD day-B-do
Collection	Colección	co-lec-see-ON
Credit	Crédito	CRAY-d-toe
Credit card	Tarjeta de crédito	tar-HEY-ta day CRAY-d-toe
Creditor	Acreedor (a)	ah-cray-a-DOOR

English	Español	Guide
Payment is now due.	El pago se debe hacer efectivo ahora.	l **PA**-go say **DAY**-bay ah-**SER** eh-fec-**T**-vo ah-**OR**-rah
It's important that we receive your payment now.	Es importante que recibamos su pago ahora.	es m-pour-**TAN**-tay kay ray-see-**BA**-mos sue **PA**-go ah-**OR**-rah
Late payment	Pago tarde	**PA**-go **TAR**-day
Past due	Pago vencido	**PA**-go ven-**SEE**-doe
When can you send your payment?	¿Cuándo puede pagar?	coo-**AN**-doe pooh-**A**-day pa-**GAR**
Interpreter	Interprete	n-**TEAR**-pray-tay
Fee	Honorario	oh-nor-**RAH**-ree-oh
Credit report	Informe de crédito	n-**FOR**-me day **CRAY**-d-tow

Here Is A Script To Help You With Collection Calls.

Hello	¡Hola!
I'm (name).	Soy (your name).
I'm from (company name).	Soy de (name of company).
I speak a little Spanish.	Hablo poco español.
Do you speak English?	¿Habla ingles?
I need to speak with ____.	Necesito hablar con señor/señora
Your account is past due.	Su cuenta está vencida.
Your payment is $.	Su pago es $.
When can you pay?	¿Cuándo puede pagar?
It's very important.	Es muy importante.
Thank you.	Gracias.

For Loan Officers

Home ownership among Latinos in the US is increasing. In order to make sure that the buyer and seller understand the complicated vocabulary in this important contract, consult the phrases below.

For more *información en español* on Fair Housing and equality in lending, contact the US Department of Housing and Urban Development (HUD) on-line at www.hud.gov. The Spanish language portion of the HUD website is great for reading practice. Researching there will also help you increase your Spanish vocabulary. If you need tax information in Spanish, go to www.irs.gov. There you can download a complete English-Spanish tax and accounting dictionary.

	English	Español	Guide
✓	Alimony	Pensión conyugal	pen-see-ON con-you-GAL
✓	Amortization	Amortización	ah-more-t-sa-see-ON
✓	Appraisal	Avalúo	ah-val-OO-oh
✓	Appraisal report	Informe de tasación	een-FOR-me day tahs-ax-see-ON
✓	Binder	Resguardo provisional	rays-goo-ARE-doe pro-v-see-oh-NAL
✓	Borrower	Prestatario	pray-sta-TAR-ree-o
✓	Buyer	Comprador	com-pra-DOOR
✓	Child support	Pensión para el suporte de niños	pen-see-ON PA-rah el soup-POUR-tay day NEEN-yos
✓	Closing	Cierre	see-A-ray
	Closing costs	Costos de cierre	CO-stows day see-A-ray

64

English	Español	Guide
Closing statement	Declaración de cierre	day-cla-rah-see-**ON** day see-**A**-ray
Co-buyer	Co-prestatario	co-pray-sta-**TAR**-ree-o
Commission	Comisión	co-me-see-**ON**
Contingency	Contingencia	con-teen-**HEN**-see-ah
Contract	Contrato	con-**TRAH**-toe
Counteroffer	Contraoferta	contra-oh-**FAIR**-ta
Covenant	Convenio	con-**VEIN**-knee-oh
Deed	Escritura de propiedad inmobiliaria	es-scree-**TOO**-rah day pro-p-a-**DAD** een-mo-b-lee-**ARE**-ree-ah
Department of Housing and Urban Development (HUD)	Departamento de la Vivienda y del Desarrollo Urbano	day-par-ta-**MEN**-toe day la v-v-**N**-da e del des-ah-**ROW**-yo oor-**BAA**-no
Discount points	Puntos de descuento	**POON**-toes day days-coo-**WAYNE**-toe
Down payment	Pago inicial	**PA**-go e-knee-see-**AL**
Earnest money	Depósito de garantía	day-**PO**-see-toe day gar-ran-**TEE**-ah
Equal Credit Opportunity Act (ECOA)	Ley de Igualdad de Oportunidad Para Obtener Crédito	lay day e-goo-al-**DAD** day oh-pour-tune-knee-**DAD** **PA**-rah ob-ten-**AIR** **CRAY**-d-toe
Escrow	Plica	**PLEE**-ca
Expenses	Gastos	**GAH**-stows

65

English	Español	Guide
FHA	Asociación Federal de Viviendas	ah-so-see-ah-see-**ON** fay-day-**RAL** day v-v-**N**-dahs
Fixed interest	Interés fija*o*	een-tay-**RACE** **FEE**-ha
Good faith estimate	Estimado de buena fe	es-t-**MA**-doe day boo-**A**-na fay
Gross annual income	Ingreso bruto anual	een-**GRAY**-so **BREW**-toe ah-new-**AL**
Gross monthly income	Ingreso bruto mensual	een-**GRAY**-so **BREW**-toe men-sue-**AL**
Hazard insurance	Seguro contra riesgos	say-**GOO**-row **CON**-tra ree-**ACE**-gos
Homeowner's insurance policy	Póliza de seguro de un propietario de vivienda	**PO**-lee-sa day say-**GOO**-row day oon pro-p-a-**TAR**-e-oh day v-v-**N**-da
In escrow	En depósito	en day-**POH**-see-toe
Interest rate	Tasa de interés	**TA**-sa day een-tay-**RES**
Monthly housing expenses	Gastos de viviendo*a* mensual	**GAS**-toes day v-v-**N**-doe men-sue-**AL**
Monthly payments	Pagos mensuales	**PA**-gos men-sue-**AL**-ace
Mortgage loan	Préstamo hipotecario	**PRAYS**-ta-mo e-poh-tay-**CAR**-e-oh
Pre-qualify	Pre-califique	pray ca-lee-**FEE**-kay
Principal and interest	Principal e interés	preen-see-**PAL** e een-tay-**RAYS**

English	Español	Guide
Private mortgage insurance	Seguro de hipoteca privado	say-GOO-row day e-po-TAY-ca pree-VA-doe
Property	Propiedad	pro-p-a-DAD
Property tax	Impuestos de propiedad	eem-poo-ES-toes day pro-p-a-DAD
Purchasing power	Poder adquisitivo	poh-DARE add-key-see-T-vo
Real estate broker	Agente de bienes raíces	ah-HEN-tay day b-N-ace rye-E-says
Remaining principal	Principal restante	preen-see-PAL ray-STAHN-tay
Seller	Vendedor	ven-day-DOOR
Term debts	Deudas a plazos	day-OO-dahs ah PLAH-sos
Title insurance	Seguro de título	say-GOO-row day TEE-too-low
Title search	Investigación del título	een-ves-t-gah-see-ON del TEE-too-low
To deduct from taxes	Deducir de los impuestos	day-do-SEER day los eem-poo-ES-toes
To quote a price	Cotizar un precio	co-t-SAR oon PRAY-see-oh
To stop making payments	Dejar de hacer pagos	day-HAR day ah-SER PA-gos
Truth In Lending Law	Ley de Veracidad en los Préstamos	lay day ver-rah-see-DAD n los PRAY-stah-mos
Veteran's Administration	Administración de Veteranos	ad-me-knees-tra-see-ON day vay-tay-RAH-nose
Work History	Historia de trabajo	east-STORE-e-ah day tra-BA-ho

Para Practicar

You are the real estate agent for the Beltrán family. Señor Beltrán wants to put in an offer of $185,000 for a home. Find out his monthly living expenses including any possible child support payments or alimony. List the vocabulary will you need below.

[Handwritten notes:]

Alimony - Pension soporte de niñas
Pension conyugal
Gastos Pagos mensuales — seguro de vida
                                      deudas a plazos
                                      carros
                                      electrodomesticos
                                      Tarjetas de credito
                                      comida
                                      vestuario
                                      gastos de transporte — gasolina
                                                                          seguros
Otros entradas
sueldo

The Tax Office
La Oficina de Impuestos

[Handwritten margin notes: IF income under a threshold no need to file / VAT]

You know the old saying: No one can escape death or taxes. Paying our local, property, state and federal taxes are a fact of life. Americans grumble about it, but realize the importance of it. What you might not realize is that other countries collect taxes in different ways. Many countries do not collect property taxes. They are levied at the time of purchase as a value added tax. Consequently, it could be the first time that your Hispanic taxpayer has ever had to pay a tax on his personal property. Be patient. Use as much Spanish as you possible to explain the amount due and what the type of tax involved.

68

English	Español	Guide
Account number	Número de cuenta	NEW-may-row day coo-**AINT**-ta
Amount	Total	toe-**TAL**
Bill	Cuenta	coo-**AINT**-ta
Bill of sale	Contrato de venta	con-**TRA**-toe day **VEN**-ta
Boat	Barco _bote_ _lancha_	**BARK**-co
Business	Negocio	nay-**GO**-see-oh
Buyer	Comprador	com-pra-**DOOR**
Camper	Autocaravana _CAMPER_	ow-toe-ca-rah-**VA**-na
Car	Carro	**CA**-row
	Auto	**OW**-toe
	Coche	**CO**-chay
Deduction	Deducción	day-duke-see-**ON**
Deed	Escritura	es-cree-**TOO**-rah
Department of Motor Vehicles	Departamento de vehículos	day-par-ta-**MEN**-toe day vay-**HE**-coo-los
Due (payable)	Vencido	ven-**SEE**-doe
Due and payable	Vencido y pagadero	ven-**SEE**-doe e pa-ga-**DAY**-row
Due in advance	Pagadero por adelantado	pa-ga-**DAY**-row pour ah-day-lahn-**TA**-doe
Due on demand	Pagadero a la vista	pa-ga-**DAY**-row ah la **VEES**-ta
Estimate	Estimación	es-t-ma-see-**ON**
Improvement	Mejora	may-**HOR**-rah
Insurance	Seguro	say-**GOO**-row
Interest	Interés	een-tay-**RES**

English	Español	Guide
Land	Tierra	t-**AIR**-rah
License plate	Placa	**PLA**-ka
Lien	Derecho de retención	day-**RAY**-cho day ray-ten-see-**ON**
Mobil home	Casa móvil	**CA**-sa **MO**-veel
Motorcycle	Motocicleta	mo-toe-see-**CLAY**-ta
Owner	Dueño	do-**WAYNE**-nyo
Personal property	Propiedad personal	pro-p-a-**DAD** pear-so-**NAL**
Property	Propiedad	pro-p-a-**DAD**
Property tax	Impuesto sobre la propiedad	m-poo-**ES**-toe **SO**-bray la pro-p-a-**DAD**
Property tax *(land)*	Contribución territorial	con-tree-boo-see-**ON** terr-ree-tor-ree-**AL**
Prorate *(n & v)*	Prorratear	pro-rah-tay-**ARE**
Real estate	Bienes raíces	b-**N**-ace rye-**EES**-ace
Refund	Reembolso	ray-m-**BOWL**-so
Registration	Registro	ray-**HEES**-tro
Resident	Residente	res-see-**DEN**-tay
RV	Vehículo de recreo	vay-**HE**-coo-lo day ray-**CRAY**-oh
Seller	Vendedor	ven-day-**DOOR**
Tax	Impuesto	m-poo-**ES**-toe
Tax collector	Recaudador de contribuciones	ray-cow-da-**DOOR** day con-tree-boo-see-**ON**-ace
Tax deductible	Deducible para efectos contributivos	day-duke-**SEE**-blay **PA**-rah a-e-**FECK**-toes con-tree-boo-**T**-vos
Tax dodging	Fraude fiscal	fur-**OW**-day fees-**KAL**

English	Español	Guide
Tax evasion	Evasión fiscal	a-vah-see-**ON** fees-**KAL**
Tax exempt	Exento de impuestos	x-**N**-toe day m-poo-**ES**-toes
Taxable value	Valor impositivo	vahl-**LORE** m-poe-see-**T**-vo
To buy	Comprar	com-**PRAR**
To make improvements on a property	Hacer mejoras a una propiedad	ah-**CER** may-**HO**-rahs ah **OO**-na pro-pee-**A**-dad
To pay	Pagar	pa-**GAR**
To sell	Vender	ven-**DARE**
Trailer	Remolque	ray-**MOLE**-kay
Truck	Camión	ca-me-**ON**
Value	Valor	va-**LORE**
Van	Furgoneta	fur-gone-**NAY**-ta
Vehicle	Vehículo	vay-**HE**-coo-lo
Vital records	Datos vitales	**DA**-toes vee-**TAL**-aces

More about Vehicles

Cars are even more expensive to purchase and to operate in Latin America than they are in the US. Owning an automobile signals the start of achieving the "American Dream" for many Latin Americans. Many auto dealerships advertise aggressively to Hispanic customers. Look around your area. Have you seen this sign? *"No crédito — No problema"!* It's one of the first big purchases many of us make — and it's one of the first times we encounter added expenses such as taxes and insurance. For those things and many others, we always remember our first car!

English	Español	Guide
What is the owner's name?	¿Cuál es el nombre del dueño?	coo-**AL** es el **NOM**-bray del doo-**WAYNE**-nyo
When did you buy the car?	¿Cuándo compró el carro?	coo-**WAND**-doe kom-**PRO** el **CA**-row
Are you buying?	¿Está comprando	es-**TA** kom-**PRAHN**-doe
Who bought the car?	¿Quién compró el carro?	key-**N** kom-**PRO** el **CA**-row
Do you have the tag?	¿Tiene la placa?	t-**N**-a la **PLAH**-ka
Did you turn in the tag?	¿Entrega la placa?	n-**TRAY**-ga la **PLAH**-ka
When?	¿Cuándo?	**KWAN**-doe
Do you have a receipt for the tag?	¿Tiene el recibo para la placa?	t-**N**-a el ray-**SEE**-bow **PAH**-rah la **PLAH**-ka
Did you sell the vehicle?	¿Vende el vehículo?	**VEIN**-day el vay-**HE**-coo-low
You need to pay the taxes	Necesita pagar los impuestos.	nay-say-**SEE**-ta pa-**GAR** los m-poo-**ES**-toes
You can make a payment plan.	Puede hacer un plan a pagar.	poo-**A**-day ah-**CER** oon plan ah pa-**GAR**
Who has vehicle?	¿Quién tiene el vehículo?	key-**N** t-**N**-a el vay-**HE**-coo-low

Types of Vehicles

English	Español	Guide
Boat	Barco	**BAR**-co
Camper	Autocaravana	**OW**-toe-ka-rah-**VA**-na
Car	Carro	**CA**-row

	English	Español	Guide
✓	Commercial vehicle	Vehículo comercial	vay-HE-coo-low co-mare-see-AL
✓	Delivery truck	Camión de reparto	ca-me-ON day ray-PAR-toe
✓	Dump truck	Volquete	vol-KAY-tay
✓	Flatbed truck	Camión de plataforma	ka-me-ON day pla-ta-FORM-ah
✓	License plate	Placa	PLAH-ka
	Pick-up truck	Camioneta	ka-me-on-NET-ta
✓	Semi-trailer	Semi-remolque	semi ray-MOLE-kay
✓	Tractor	Tractor	trac-TOR
✓	Tractor trailer	Camión tractor	ka-me-ON trac-TOR
✓	Trailer	Remolque	ray-MOLE-kay
✓	Van	Furgoneta	fur-gone-NET-ta

Para Practicar
Señor Vargas has purchased a used vehicle .Can you ask him the following questions?

1. What is your complete name? _____

2. What is your address? _____

3. Did you purchase a car or a truck? _____

4. On what date did you purchase the vehicle? _____
    _____

5. Do you have the tag? _____

6. The tax is $31.44 _____

73

Property Taxes

Home ownership is the goal of most Americans. In this respect, Latin Americans are no different. Many begin the path to home ownership by renting and saving to make their purchase. Often they will work second jobs to reach their goal.

Saving is a big part of Latin American culture. It's an important concept that begins in childhood. When a child is born, relatives buy piggy banks for the youngster. On every visit the child is given some coins to put in the bank to save. The money is used for expenses later like the 15th birthday celebration for girls called the "*quinceañeros.*" It can also be used for college savings. As a result of this lifelong commitment to saving, many Latinos have cash reserves for down payments on property. Over the past few years home ownership among Latinos has greatly increased. It's a trend that you will see continue in the years to come.

English	Español	Guide
Bill of sale	Contracto de venta	con-TRAC-toe day vein-TA
Do you have a contract for a deed?	¿Tiene un contrato para una escritura?	t-N-a oon con-TRAC-toe PA-rah OO-na es-cree-TOO-rah
Do you have a land contract?	¿Tiene un contrato para tierra?	t-N-a oon con-TRAC-toe PA-rah t-AIR-rah
Do you have a tax bill?	¿Tiene una factura de impuestos?	t-N-a OO-na fac-TOO-rah day eem-poo- ES-toes
Do you need a Tax Card? (Appraisal Sheet)	¿Necesita una tarjeta para calcular impuestos?	nay-say-SEE-ta OO-na tar-HEY-ta PA-rahcal-coo-LAR m-poo- ES-toes

English	Español	Guide
Is it a Mobile home? Doublewide? Manufactured Housing?	Es una Casa móvil Casa móvil doble Casa fabricada	es OO-na CA-sa MO-veel CA-sa MO-veel DOE-blay CA-sa fa-bree-CA-da
Is it real estate or personal property?	¿Es bienes raíces o propiedad personal?	es b-N-es rye-EE-ace oh pro-pee-a-DAD pear-so-NAL
The tax value is.	El valor para impuestos es	el vah-LORE m-poo-ES-toes-es
What is the parcel identification number?	¿Cuál es el número de identificación de la parcela?	coo-ALL es el NEW-may-row day e-den-t-fee-ka-see-ON day la par-SAY-la
When did you buy the property?	¿Cuándo compró la propiedad?	KWAN-doe kom-PRO la pro-p-a-DAD

Para Practicar

What would you say in each of the following situations?

1. Tell Señor Hernandez the tax value of his property is $1277.95.

_____

2. Ask Señor Valasquez if he has a bill of sale.

_____

3. Ask Señor Rodriguez when he bought his property.

_____

Tax Vocabulary for CPAs

US government websites are excellent resources for Spanish vocabulary. The IRS is particularly strong in this area. Preparing taxes can be extremely tedious and frustrating for both parties. To help you get a good start, we have selected the most common terms used in tax collection and preparation. For more terms go online to the IRS website: www.irs.gov. In the search field, ask for Publication 850. This is a complete English–Spanish glossary of tax terms. Make a copy of this handy publication and keep it at your desk so it will be prepared when a Spanish-speaking customer needs your assistance.

English	Español	Guide
Ability to pay	Capacidad de pago	c-pa-see-**DAD** de **PA**-go
Accrued taxes	Contribuciones acumuladas	con-tree-boo-see-**ON**-ace ah-coo-moo-**LA**-das
Applicant	Solicitante	so-lee-see-**TAN**-tay
Arrears	Mora	**MORE**-ra
Assets	Bienes	b-**N**-ace
Back taxes	Impuestos atrasados	m-poo-**ES**-toes ah-tra-**SA**-dose
Capital assets	Bienes de capital	b-**N**-ace day ca-p-**TAL**
Cash	Efectivo	a-fec-**T**-vo
Cashier's check	Cheque de caja	**CHE**-kay day **CA**-ha
Deferred taxes	Impuestos diferidos	m-poo-**ES**-toe d-fer-**REE**-dose

English	Español	Guide
Delinquent tax	Impuesto debido y no pagado	m-poo-**ES**-toe day-**B**-doe e no pa-**GA**-doe
Demand for payment	Requerimiento de pago	ray-care-ree-me-**N**-toe day **PA**-go
Equity	Valor neto del derecho	va-**LORE NAY**-to del day-**RAY**-cho
Estate tax	Impuesto sobre la herencia	m-poo-**ES**-toe **SO**-bray la air-**WREN**-see-ah
Estimated tax	Impuesto estimado	m-poo-**ES**-toe es-t-**MA**-doe
Face value	Valor nominal	va-**LORE** no-me-**NAL**
Failure to pay penalty	Multa por no pagar	**MOOL**-ta pour no pa-**GAR**
Fair market value	Valor normal en el Marcado	va-**LORE** nor-**MAL** en l mar-**CA**-doe
Tax lien	Gravamen por impuesto	gra-va-**MEN** pour m-poo- **ES**-toe
Fees	Honorarios	on-no-**RAHR**-e-ohs
Finance charge	Costo por financiamiento	**CO**-stow pour fee-nan-see-ah-me-**N**-toe
Franchise	Franquicia	fran-**KEY**-see-ah
Gross income	Ingreso bruto	een-**GRAY**-so **BREW**-toe
Incur a penalty	Incurrir una multa	n-coo-**REAR** **OO**-na **MOOL**-ta
Independent contractor	Contratista independiente	con-tra-**T**-sta n-d-pen-d-**N**-tay
Interest rate	Tasa de interés	**TA**-sa day een-tay-**RES**

English	Español	Guide
Late payment penalty	Multa por mora	MOOL-ta pour MORE-ah
Make payment to	Hacer pagadero a	ah-SER pa-ga-DAY-row ah
Minimum payment	Pago mínimo	PA-go ME-knee-mo
Money order	Giro	HE-row
Monthly payments	Pagos mensuales	PA-gos men-sue-AHL-ace
Mortgage	Hipoteca	e-po-TEK-ca
Net income	Ingreso neto	m-poo-ES-toe NE-toe
Notice of levy	Notificación de embargo	no-t-fee-ca-see-ON day m-BAR-go
Over payment	Pago en exceso	PA-go in x-SAY-so
Penalty	Multa	MOOL-ta
Personal property	Propiedad personal	pro-p-a-DAD pear-so-NAL
Real estate	Bienes inmuebles	b-N-ace n-moo-A-blays
Real estate tax	Impuesto sobre bienes inmuebles	m-poo- ES-toe SO-bray b-N- es n-moo-A-blays
Sales tax	Impuesto sobre ventas	m-poo- ES-toe SO-bray VEIN-tas
Sole proprietor	Dueño único	do-WAYNE-yo OO-knee-co
Tax	Impuesto	m-poo- ES-toe
Tax Bill	Factura de impuestos	fac-TOO-rah day m-poo- ES-toes
Tax credit	Crédito tributario	CRAY-d-toe tree-boo-TAR-ree-oh

English	Español	Guide
Tax exemption	Exención del impuesto	x-n-see-**ON** del m-poo-**ES**-toe
Tax liability	Impuesto por pagar	m-poo-**ES**-toe pour pa-**GAR**
Tax penalty	Multa por impuestos	**MOOL**-ta pour m-poo-**ES**-toes
Tax rate	Tasa de impuesto	**TA**-sa day m-poo-**ES**-toe
Underpayment	Pago insuficiente	**PA**-go n-sue-fee-see-**N**-tay
Wages	Salarios	sa-**LAR**-ree-ohs

Para Practicar

In the space below, write the eight words from the previous sections that you will use the most at work. Then, write them on an index card or "sticky" note. Keep your "cheat-sheet" with you and refer to it often. Read through it at least twice each day. This technique will help you learn the words faster — and provide a reference for you when you need them at work.

1. _____

2. _____

3. _____

4. _____

5. _____

6. _____

7. _____

8. _____

In the Store — En la tienda

American retailers are recognizing the importance of Hispanic shoppers for a variety of reasons. Currently, Latino purchasing power in the US is estimated at over 700 billion dollars annually — now that's *mucho dinero*! That number is expected to rise to the one trillion dollar mark within a few years. Latinos are widely known for being extremely loyal customers. In stores where Spanish is spoken, Hispanic customers feel respected, valued and have a positive shopping experience. Many of them consider the extra courtesy a more powerful draw than low prices.

If you have an opportunity to watch Spanish language channels on television, begin to notice how many companies you recognize that air commercials in Spanish. This is a super opportunity for you to see how large firms market to their Spanish-speaking customers. You'll be surprised at what you learn by being observant. The following list will get you started with the basics.

English	Español	Guide
Aisle	Pasillo	pa-SEE-yo
Anything else?	Algo más	AL-go mahs
Application	Solicitud	so-lee-see-TOOD
Come with me.	Venga con migo.	VEIN-ga con-ME-go
Credit	Crédito	CRAY-d-toe
Discount	Descuenta	days-coo-WAYNE-ta
Job opening	Posición vacante	po-see-zee-ON va-CAN-tay
I need to exchange this.	Necesito cambiar esto.	nay-say-SEE-toe cam-b-ARE ES-toe
I need to place an order.	Necesito poner una orden.	nay-say-SEE-toe pone-AIR OO-na OR-den

English	Español	Guide
I need to return this.	Necesito devolver esto.	nay-say-**SEE**-toe day-vol-**VAIR** **ES**-toe
In stock	En acción	n ax-see-**ON**
May I help you?	¿Puedo ayudarle?	poo-**A**-doe eye-you-**DAR**-lay
Outlet store	Tienda de ventas a descuento	t-**N**-da day **VEIN**-tas ah des-coo-**WAYNE**-toe
Out of stock	No es en acción	no es n ax-see-**ON**
Order form	Hoja de pedido	**OH**-ja day pay-**D**-doe
Sale	Venta	**VEIN**-ta
We can order it quickly.	Podemos pedirlo pronto.	po-**DAY**-mos pay-**DEAR**-low **PRON**-toe
We don't have that.	No tenemos esto.	no tay-**NAY**-mos **ES**-toe
What do you need?	¿Qué necesita?	**KAY** nay-say-**SEE**-ta

Para Practicar

1. Señora de la Jara is purchasing an item that costs $57.98. She pays you in cash with $60. Using your Spanish, count her change and ask if there is anything else you can help with.

2. You work in an electronics store. Señor Carillo wants to purchase a computer, but it is out of stock. Tell him that the computer is out of stock, but that you can order it and it will arrive tomorrow. Also tell him that the computer is on sale at a 30% discount.

3. A Latino family has entered your store to buy a camera. Tell them to come with you and on which aisle the item is located. Also tell them that the item is on sale for a 40% discount

Talking with Customers

As you continue to work with Hispanic customers, you will want to learn more and more vocabulary. To facilitate the learning process, think critically about your store and the merchandise it carries. Also think about how you personally interact with customers. What questions do they ask you? Answering questions like these will help you prioritize your vocabulary so you will know what to say in any retail situation.

English	Español	Guide
Advertisement	Anuncio	ah-**NOON**-see-oh
As is	Como está	**CO**-mo es-**TA**
Bargain	Ganga	**GANG**-ah
Billboard	Cartelera	car-tay-**LAY**-rah
Brand	Marca	**MAR**-ca
Cashier	Cajero *(a)*	ca-**HAIR**-row
Change	Cambio	**CAM**-b-oh
Charge	Cargo	**CAR**-go
Closed	Cerrado	ser-**RAH**-doe
Customer	Cliente	clee-**N**-tay
Direct mail	Correo directo	co-**RAY**-oh d-**WRECK**-toe
Discount	Descuento	des-**KWAYNE**-toe
Down payment	Pago inicial	**PA**-go e-knee-see-**AL**
Installment	Plazo	**PLA**-so
Mail order	Pedido por correo	pay-**D**-doe pour core-**RAY**-oh
Manager	Gerente	hey-**RENT**-tay

English	Español	Guide
Merchandise	Mercancía	mer-cahn-**SEE**-ah
Money	Dinero	d-**NAY**-row
Open	Abierta	ah-**B**-air-ta
Paid-in-full	Pagado en su totalidad	pa-**GA**-doe in su to-ta-lee-**DAD**
Price	Precio	**PRAY**-see-oh
Price reduction	Reducción de precio	ray-duke-see-**ON** day **PRAY**-see-oh
Product	Producto	pro-**DUKE**-toe
Receipt	Recibo	ray-**SEE**-bo
Refund	Reembolso	ray-m-**BOWL**-so
Retail	Al por menor	al pour **MAY**-nor
Return	Devolución	day-vo-lou-see-**ON**
Rush order	Pedido urgente	pay-**D**-do oor-**HEN**-tay
Sale	Venta	**VEN**-ta
Sales tax	Impuesto de venta	m-poo- **ES**-toe day **VEIN**-ta
Sales person	Vendedor	ven-day-**DOOR**
	Vendedora	ven-day-**DOOR**-ah
Sample	Muestra	moo-**ES**-tra
Self-service	Auto servicio	**OW**-toe ser-**V**-see-oh
Subtotal	Subtotal	soob-toe-**TAL**
Sum	Suma	**SUE**-ma
Total	Total	toe-**TAL**
Used	Usado	oo-**SA**-doe
Wholesale	Al por mayor	al pour my-**ORE**

Taking Orders

Talking on the telephone in a new language requires practice, patience, and preparation. The more organized you are about what you need to say— nd what you expect to hear, the more successful you will be. In many instances taking orders by phone follows a routine pattern. You ask for the same information from each customer to complete their order. Take a moment to think critically about the questions you ask during each transaction, and write a script in Spanish containing this important vocabulary. Keep your notes at your desk so that you can find them at a moment's notice! After each call, take a moment to think about how it went. Did you use the phrases you thought you would need? Were there words or phrases you needed and didn't include? Make new list immediately after you've finished the call when the conversation is fresh in your mind reference guide. Being prepared will go a long way toward building your confidence — and that's critical to your success with this important task.

English	Español	Guide
Would you like?	¿Le gustaría?	lay goo-star-**REE**-ah
Buy it	Cómprelo	**COM**-pray-low
Charge it	Cárguelo	**CAR**-gay-low
Deliver it	Entréguelo	in-**TRAY**-gay-low
Exchange it	Cámbielo	**CAM**-b-a-low
Get it	Consígalo	con-**SEE**-ga-low
Pay it	Páguelo	**PA**-gay-low
Pick it up	Recójalo	ray-co-**HA**-low
Return it	Devuélvalo	day-voo-**L**-va-low
Sell it	Véndalo	**VEN**-da-low
Send it	Mándelo	**MAN**-day-low
Sign it	Fírmelo	**FEAR**-may-low
What is the problem with your order?	¿Cuál es el problema con su orden?	coo-**AL** es l pro-**BLAY**-ma con sue **OR**-den

Methods of Payment

English	Español	Guide
We accept	Aceptamos	ah-sep-**TA**-mos
Cash	Efectivo	a-fec-**T**-vo
Cashier's checks	Cheques bancarios	**CHECK**-ace ban-**CAR**-ree-ohs
Checks	Cheques	**CHECK**-ace
Credit cards	Tarjetas de crédito	tar-**HEY**-tas day **CRAY**-d-toes
Money order	Orden de pago	**OR**-den day **PA**-go
Postal money order	Giro postal	**HE**-row pos-**TAL**

Tips & Tidbits:

When talking on the telephone to customers who speak Spanish, keep a list of vocabulary words you will need on index cards at your desk. Review them often. Good customer service comes through no matter what language you speak!

On the Telephone

Talking on the telephone with Spanish-speaking customers is one of the most challenging skills to develop. There's no body language or facial expression from your customer to help you. The best way to start this process is to stay as organized as possible. Think carefully about the kind of calls you make to your English speaking customers. What are the phrases you say most often and the typical responses from your customers? Learn these phrases first. Remember it is better to use some of the phrases from page 15 to help you if you get in a jam. There's nothing wrong with saying, *"Repeta, por favor. Habla más despacio."* Make a script to help you get started with telephone skills. This will help you build your confidence.

English	Español	Guide
800 number	Número de ochocientos	NEW-may-row day OH-cho-see-N-toes
Answering machine	Contestador telefónico	con-tes-TA-door tay-lay-FOE-knee-co
Area code	Código de área	CO-d-go day AH-ray-ah
Ask for this number.	Pida este número.	p-da ES-tay NEW-may-row
Cellular phone	Teléfono celular El cel	tay-lay-FOE-no say-YOU-lar el cell
Collect call	Llamada a cobro revertido	ya-MA-da ah CO-bro ray-ver-T-doe
Conference call	Llamada de conferencia	ya-MA-da de con-fer-WRENN-see-ah
Could you call later?	¿Puede llamar más tarde?	poo-A-day ya-MAR mas TAR-day
Dial this number.	Marque este número.	MAR-quc ES-tay NEW-may-row
Extension	Extensión	x-ten-see-ON
Fax	Facsímile	fax-SEE-meal
Hang up the telephone.	Cuelgue el teléfono.	coo-L-gay el tay-LAY-foe-no
He/She isn't here.	No está aquí.	no es-TA ah-KEY
He/she will call back later.	Llamará más tarde.	ya-MAR-rah MAS tar-DAY
Headset	Auriculares con micrófono	ow-ree-coo-LAR-es con me-CROW-foe-no
Hold a moment,	Espere un momento.	es-PEAR-ray oon mo-MEN-toe

English	Español	Guide
I have the wrong number.	Tengo el número equivocado.	**TANG**-go el **NEW**-may-row a-key-vo-**CA**-doe
I'd like to leave a message.	Me gustaría dejar un mensaje.	may goo-star-**REE**-ah day-**HAR** oon men-**SA**-je
I'll transfer you to	Le voy a transferir a	lay voy a trans-fair-**REAR** ah
I'm calling about ____.	Estoy llamando acerca de ____.	es-**TOY** ya-**MAHN**-doe ah-**SER**-ca day
Is this the correct number?	¿Es el número correcto?	es el **NEW**-may-row co-**WRECK**-toe
It's very important.	Es muy importante.	es mooy m-pour-**TAHN**-tay
Local call	Llamada local	ya-**MA**-da low-**CAL**
Long distance	Larga distancia	**LAR**-ga dees-**TAN**-see-ah
May I speak to ____?	¿Puedo hablar con ____?	poo-**A**-doe ah-**BLAR** con ____
Press this number.	Oprima este número.	oh-**PRE**-ma **ES**-tay **NEW**-may-row
Repeat that please.	Repítelo, por favor	ray-**P**-tay-low pour fa-**VOR**
Switchboard	Conmutador	con-moo-ta-**DOOR**
Telephone number	Número de teléfono	**NEW**-may-row day tay-**LAY**-foe-no
The connection is bad.	La conexión está mala.	la co-nex-see-**ON** es-**TA MA**-la
The line is busy.	La línea está ocupada.	la **LEE**-nay-ah es-**TA** oh-coo-**PA**-da

English	Español	Guide
The number is disconnected.	El número está desconectado.	el **NEW**-may-row es-**TA** des-co-neck-**TA**-da
There is a phone call for	Hay una llamada para _____.	eye **OO**-na ya-**MA**-da **PA**-ra _____.
Two-way radio	Radioteléfono portátil	ra-d-oh-tay-**LAY**-foe-no pour-**TA**-teel
Wait for the tone.	Espere por el tono.	es-**PEAR**-ray pour el **TOE**-no
Would you like to leave a message?	¿Le gustaría dejar un mensaje?	lay goo-star-**REE**-ah day-**HAR** oon men-**SA**-he
You have the wrong number.	Tiene el número equivocado.	t-**N**-a l **NEW**-may-row a-key-vo-**CA**-doe
Your name, please	Su nombre, por favor	sue **NOM**-brey pour fa-**VOR**
Your number, please	Su número, por favor	sue **NEW**-may-row pour fa-**VOR**

Tips & Tidbits

Employees with different cultural backgrounds will have different attitudes towards work and employers that will have an impact on your management style. According to Eva S. Kras in her book *Management in Two Cultures* (Intercultural Press, 1995) Latin Americans are less likely to report an on-the-job injury than American employees. In many areas south of the border workers are essentially trained to tell the boss what he *wants* to hear rather than what he *needs* to hear. Many Latin Americans fear that they will be fired if they become injured on the job— or if they are handling a piece of equipment that breaks. Training is the key to managing these issues. Use your Spanish to help you build open relationships that keep lines of communication open.

Clothing — La Ropa

All types of clothing and clothing stores are found in Latin America. The diversity is endless. There are outdoor markets or *mercados*, where buyers haggle to get the best prices, to upper end, designer stores in larger cities. In many Latin American countries, people tend to dress less casually than in the US. There are many places south of the border where jeans and tee-shirts are just not appropriate! The love of style and fashion will certainly bring customers into your store.

There's one special occasion that causes everyone to dress up. That's the celebration of a young lady's fifteenth birthday or *quinceañera* (**KEEN**-say-ahn-**YER**-ah). The *quinceañera* party marks the time when a girl becomes a young lady. Large parties mark the event with music, dancing and great food. A confirmation service at the family's church can also mark the celebration. In many families, no expense is spared for the dress the young lady wears at the party. It is often white, formal, and adorned with delicate lace. Even though a white dress is traditional, pastel colors are also used. Some families begin a savings account when the child is born that is ear-marked especially for the *quinceañera* celebration. Truly it is one of the biggest experiences in a young lady's life!

English	Español	Guide
Bathing suit	Traje de baño	**TRAH**-hey day **BAHN**-yo
Belt	Cinturón	seen-too-**RHONE**
Blouse	Blusa	**BLUE**-sa
Boots	Botas	**BOW**-tas
Dress	Vestido	ves-**T**-doe
Gloves	Guantes	goo-**AHN**-tays
Handkerchief	Pañuelo	pah-new-**A**-low
Hat	Sombrero	som-**BRAY**-row

English	Español	Guide
Jacket	Chaqueta	cha-**KAY**-ta
Jeans	Jeans	Jeans
	Vaqueros	va-**KAY**-rows
Overcoat	Abrigo	ah-**BREE**-go
Pants	Pantalones	pan-ta-**LONE**-ace
Pajamas	Pijamas	p-**HA**-mas
Raincoat	Impermeable	eem-pear-may-**AH**-blay
Robe	Bata	**BA**-ta
Sandals	Sandalias	san-**DAL**-e-ahs
Scarf	Bufanda	boo-**FAHN**-da
Shirt	Camisa	ca-**ME**-sa
Shoes	Zapatos	sa-**PA**-toes
Shorts	Pantalones cortos	pan-ta-**LONE**-ace **CORE**-toes
Skirt	Falda	**FALL**-da
Sneakers	Tenis	**TAY**-knees
Socks	Calcetines	cal-say-**TEEN**-ace
Suit	Traje	**TRAH**-hey
Sweater	Suéter	sue-**A**-ter
Tie	Corbata	core-**BA**-ta
T-shirt	Camiseta	ca-me-**SET**-ta
Umbrella	Paraguas	**PA**-ra-**AH**-goo-wahs
Underwear	Ropa interior	**ROW**-pa een-tay-ree-**OR**
Vest	Chaleco	cha-**LAY**-co

Tips & Tidbits

1. Dollars and cents are ***dólares y centavos*** (DOE-lar-es e cen-TA-vos). Think back to what you learned about the Spanish sound system. Why does the Spanish word for dollar only have one "*l*"? You're right! The "*ll*" is one of four additional letters in the Spanish alphabet and it always sounds like an English "*y*."

2. For the Hispanic consumer, price isn't always the driving factor in where they choose to shop. According to a Nielsen study in 2002, Hispanic consumer's reasons for deciding where to shop were: freshness, cleanliness, friendly employees, low prices, and high quality. Hispanic customers equate the ability to speak Spanish with friendliness.

3. Hispanics more often spend their money on:

    a. Groceries

    b. Footwear

    c. Men's and children's

    d. Clothing

    e. Gasoline

    f. Telephone services

Sizes and Styles — Tamaños y Estilos

English	Español	Guide
I need a size	Necesito un tamaño	nay-say-see-toe oon ta-**MAHN**-yo
Small	Pequeño	pay-**CAIN**-yo
Medium	Mediano	may-d-**AH**-no
Large	Grande	**GRAHN**-day
Extra large	Extra grande	X-tra **GRAHN**-day

English	Español	Guide
I like it a lot.	Me gusta mucho.	may **GOO**-sta **MOO**-cho
It fits me.	Me queda. *bim*	may **KAY**-da
It doesn't fit me.	No me queda bien.	no may **KAY**-da b-N
It's OK.	Está bien.	es-**TA** b-N
It's practical.	Es práctico (a).	es **PRAC**-t-co
It's small.	Es pequeño.	es pay-**CAIN**-yo
It's tight.	Es apretado.	es ah-pray-**TA**-doe
It's short.	Es corto.	es **CORE**-toe
It's long.	Es largo.	es **LAR**-go
It's narrow.	Es estrecho.	es ace-**TRAY**-cho

Colors

English	Español	Guide
Black	Negro	**NAY**-grow
Blue	Azul	**AH**-sool
Brown	Café	ca-**FAY**
Dark	Oscuro	oh-**SKOO**-row
Green	Verde	**VER**-day
Grey	Gris	grease
Pale	Pálido	**PA**-lee-doe
Pink	Rosa	**ROW**-sa
Purple	Morado	mo-**RAH**-do
Red	Rojo	**ROW**-ho
Solid	Sólido	**SO**-lee-doe
White	Blanco	**BLAHN**-co
Yellow	Amarillo	ah-ma-**REE**-yo

Discounts and Sales

English	Español	Guide
Welcome	Bienvenidos	b-N-veh-**KNEE**-dose
Are there any sales?	¿Hay ventas?	eye **VEIN**-tas
Are there discounts?	¿Hay descuentos?	eye des-coo-**WAYNE**-toes
Is someone helping you?	¿Los están atendiendo?	los es-**TAN** ah-ten-knee-N-doe
What would you like?	¿Qué desea?	kay day-**SAY**-ah
What are you looking for?	¿Para qué está buscando?	**PA**-rah kay es-**TA** boos-**CAHN**-doe
I'm looking for a	Estoy buscando un (una)	es-**TOY** boos-**CAHN**-doe oon/**OO**-na
How many do you need?	¿Cuántos necesita?	**KWAN**-tose nay-say-**SEE**-ta
Is there something else?	¿Algo más?	**AL**-go mas
May I help you?	¿Puedo servirle?	poo-**A**-doe seer-**VEER**-lay
This is the payment plan.	Este es el plan de pagos.	**ES**-tay es el plan day **PA**-gos
We don't have any more.	No tenemos más.	no tay-**NAY**-mos mas
We don't sell them anymore.	Ya no los vendemos.	ya no los ven-**DAY**-mos
Which one do you like?	¿Cuál le gusta?	coo-**AHL** lay **GOO**-sta
Which one do you want?	¿Cuál quiere?	coo-**AHL** key-**AIR**-ray
Thanks for coming in today.	Gracias por venir hoy.	**GRA**-see-ah por veh-**NEAR** oy
Come back soon.	Regrese pronto.	ray-**GRAY**-say **PRON**-toe

93

1. Since 2001, Hispanic disposable income has increased over 29%. That's over two times the growth amount of the general US consumer.

2. In 2010 the disposable income in Hispanic households is expected to top one trillion dollars.

3. 69% of foreign born Hispanics prefer shopping in stores where employees speak Spanish.
   (*Ahorre Marketing, 2005*)

4. "Hispanic shopping and spending levels increase with acculturation. Service, familiarity and employee friendliness also influence purchases."
   (*El Mercado Minorista, December 2005*)

5. Hispanic shoppers respond positively to the extra attention shown to them by Spanish-speaking employees.

6. Get your message out by advertising in Spanish language newspapers and on Spanish language radio stations in your area. Advertising in Spanish-language media outlets is a sure way to bring in new customers.

In the Department Store

Stores in Latin America provide a variety of items and shopping experiences just as they do in the United States; however the shopping habits of your Spanish–

speaking customers could be slightly different. Since shopping is a social occasion everyone enjoys — for many Hispanic families going shopping involves the *entire* family. Trips to the store for groceries or household items usually include everyone from the youngest child to granny and granddad. These family shopping excursions usually take place on weekends or in the evening after work. Your Hispanic customers may also prefer to pay for their purchases in cash rather than with personal checks or credit cards.

Large Latin American cities feature all kinds of large department and specialty stores. In these stores prices or discounts are clearly marked. Latin American department stores, *el almacén* usually provide the same sort of shopping experience that one finds anywhere in the United States. You will be able to make your purchases faster and you'll find a larger inventory on hand. US chain stores that have locations in Latin America also feature a very consistent store layout and product line. It makes for a very comfortable shopping experience because all the items are where you expect them to be.

In some Latin American specialty stores customer service is a real treat. It is very personal, and the customer is pampered with *mucha atención*. The sales person will greet you as you enter the store and will stay with you as long as you are in the store, in case you need any help. That's real VIP treatment! So, make sure to greet your Spanish-speaking customers when they enter the store and offer to be of service. Every consumer, no matter what their culture or background, appreciates being in a comfortable atmosphere where their patronage is valued.

In rural areas of Latin America shopping is more traditional. Open-air markets like our "flea markets" are typical. Bargaining for the best price is often expected and enjoyed in these *mercados*. It's not unusual to go to one "stand" to purchase fruits, go to another for milk, and go on to others for meat or other household items. This section contains vocabulary for various sections in a department store. Learning this vocabulary will help you direct Spanish–speaking customers to specific places in your store. If you hear the phrase, *"¿Dónde está?"* your customer is asking you "where is"?

English	Español	Guide
Aisle	Pasillo	pa-**SEE**-yo
Appliances	Aparatos	ah-par-**RAH**-toes
Automotive	Automotor	ow-toe-mo-**TOR**
Baby strollers	Cochecillos	co-chay-**SEE**-yos
Batteries	Batería	ba-ter-**REE**-ah
Blanket	Manta	**MAHN**-ta

English	Español	Guide
Books	Libros	**LEE**-bros
Camping	Acampada	ah-cam-**PA**-da
Children's clothing	Ropa de niños	**ROW**-pa day **KNEE**-nyos
Children's furniture	Muebles infantiles	moo-**A**-blays een-fahn-**TEAL**-es
Clothes	Ropa	**ROW**-pa
Cosmetics	Cosméticos	cos-**MAY**-t-cos
Crystal	Cristal	crease-**TAL**
Curtains	Cortinas	core-**T**-nahs
Customer service	Servicios al cliente	ser-**V**-see-ohs al clee-**N**-tay
Diapers	Pañales	pahn-**YAL**-es
Dishes	Vajillas	va-**HE**-yas
Electronics	Electrónicas	a-lec-**TRON**-knee-cas
Elevator	Ascensor	ah-sen-**SOAR**
Exit	Salida	sa-**LEE**-da
Fishing rods	Caña de pescar	**CAN**-ya day pes-**CAR**
Food	Comida	co-**ME**-da
Furniture	Muebles	moo-**A**-blays
Garden	Jardín	har-**DEAN**
Hardware	Ferretería	fair-ray-ter-**REE**-ah
Health and beauty	Salud y belleza	sa-**LEWD** e bay-**YEA**-sa
Hobbies	Pasatiempos	**PA**-sa-t-**M**-pos
Housewares	Efectos de domicilio	a-**FEC**-toes day do-me-**SEE**-lee-oh

English	Español	Guide
Jewelry	Joyería	hoy-yea-**REE**-ah
Lamps	Lámparas	**LAM**-pa-rahs
Lost and Found	Oficina de objetos perdidos	oh-fee-**SEE**-na day ob-**HEY**-toes pear-**D**-dose
Luggage	Equipaje	a-key-**PA**-hey
Magazines	Revistas	ray-**V**-stahs
Men's clothing	Ropa de caballeros	**ROW**-pa day ca-baa-**YAIR**-rows
Music	Música	**MOO**-see-ca
Optical	Óptica	**OHP**-t-ca
Paint	Pintura	peen-**TOO**-rah
Pans	Cacerolas	ca-say-**ROW**-las
Pets	Mascotas	mas-**CO**-tahs
Pharmacy	Farmacia	far-**MA**-see-ah
Photo Center	Fotografía	fo-toe-**GRA**-fee-ah
Plants	Plantas	**PLAN**-tas
Pots	Ollas	**OH**-yas
Sheets	Sábanas	**SA**-ba-nas
Shoes	Zapatos	sa-**PA**-toes
Television	Televisor	tay-lay-v-**SOAR**
Tools	Herramientas	air-rah-me-**N**-tas
Towels	Toallas	toe-**EYE**-yas
Toys	Juguetes	who-**GET**-tays
Women's clothing	Ropa de dama	**ROW**-pa day **DAH**-ma

Tips & Tidbits

1. The Hispanic population is growing faster than any other market segment.

2. The younger generation of Hispanic consumers is driving the retail market. 60% of the Hispanic market is below the age of 30 and almost twice as likely to live in households of four or more people.

3. To attract Hispanic customers it's important to hire Hispanic employees, display bilingual signage in your store, distribute bilingual coupons, and increase your product line to include items which appeal to Hispanic consumers.

4. Look to the future. Economists are predicting that the Hispanic population boom during the first two decades of the 2000s will have approximately the same magnitude of impact on the US marketplace as the Baby Boomers of the 1950s and 1960s did.

In the Grocery Store

Hispanic tastes in foods and beverages are influencing the items we see on supermarket shelves every day. In many Central and South American countries the variety of fresh fruits and vegetables is astounding. As a result of the growing Hispanic population who are familiar with these healthy, tasty foods, more tropical varieties are being imported into the US and selections in the "ethnic" aisle are growing.

According to several marketing surveys, Latin Americans tend to use more fresh fruits and vegetables than other consumers. They often prepare meals at home during the week and go out for meals on the weekend. During the week they usually make several trips to the grocery store. This typical buying habit keeps the produce they purchase fresher, because they buy only what they need for a day or two.

English	Español	Guide
Beans	Frijoles	free-**HO**-les
Beef	Carne de vaca	**CAR**-nay day **VA**-ca
	Carne de rez	**CAR**-nay day rez
Beer	Cerveza	ser-**VAY**-sa
Bread	Pan	pahn
Butter	Mantequilla	mahn-tay-**KEY**-ya
Cake mix	Harina preparada para pastel	ah-**REE**-na pre-par-**RAH**-da **PA**-rah pas-**TEL**
Canned goods	Alimentos enlatados	ah-lee-**MEN**-toes n-la-**TA**-dose
Canned vegetables	Vegetales enlatados	vay-he-**TAL**-es n-la-**TA**-dose
Cereal	Cereal	say-ree-**AL**
Cheese	Queso	**KAY**-so
Convenience food	Platos preparados	**PLA**-toes pray-pa-**RA**-does
Cookie	Galleta	ga-**YEA**-ta
Detergent	Detergente	day-ter-**HEN**-tay
Drinks	Bebidas	bay-**B**-dahs
Eggs	Huevos	oo-**WAVE**-ohs
Fish	Pescado	pes-**CA**-does
Flowers	Flores	**FLOOR**-res
Freezer	Congelador	con-hell-ah-**DOOR**
Fruit	Fruta	**FRU**-ta
Ice-cream	Helado	a-**LA**-doe
Juice	Jugo	**WHO**-go

English	Español	Guide
Lard	Manteca	man-TAKE-ah
Meat	Carne	CAR-nay
Milk	Leche	LAY-che
Oil	Aceite	ah-SAY-tay
Pasta	Fideo	fee-DAY-oh
Poultry	Carne de ave	CAR-nay day AH-vay
Produce	Productos del campo	pro-DUKE-toes del CAM-po
Rice	Arroz	ah-ROS
Snacks	Aperitivos	ah-pear-ree-T-vos
Soup	Sopa	SO-pa
Vegetables	Vegetales	vay-he-TAL-es
Wine	Vino	V-no

Tips & Tidbits

1. Hispanics tend to buy more fresh produce and meats than other segments of the population. They also eat out less frequently.

2. A recent online study of the Hispanic population's taste preferences in beverages and sweets found that a high percentage preferred fruit flavors. Latinos tend to enjoy fruit-flavored sodas over colas. Here is a list of the most popular fruit flavors: Pineapple, mango, watermelon, strawberry, citrus and grape.

A Little More Direction

In front	En frente
At the back	Al fondo
Thanks	Gracias
Here's your change.	Aquí está su vuelto

In the Guest's Room
En la Habitación del Huesped

Customer service can take a variety of forms in the hospitality industry. You will use Spanish with guests at your property, as well as with members of your staff. This vocabulary is very practical to know when you are traveling yourself!

Here are the names of common items found in a hotel guest's room. Each hotel has its own cleaning and maintenance routine. Think about how the rooms on your property are maintained and list the amenities they contain. To help everyone learn this essential vocabulary, label an empty room with sticky notes in English and Spanish. Urge members of your staff to go to that room and run through the vocabulary as often as possible. If it's not possible to label an actual guest's room, post five new words each week in both languages in your break room. Everyone can learn together. This practice exercise is great for team-building and it sends a clear message to the entire staff about the importance of learning Spanish in a business setting.

I need to clean your room, please.
Necesito limpiar su cuarto, por favor.

English	Español	Guide
Air conditioning	Aire acondicionado	EYE-ray ah-con-d-see-oh-**NA**-doe
Bath tub	Bañera	ban-**YEA**-rah
Bathroom	Baño	**BAN**-yo
Bed	Cama	**KA**-ma
Bed spread	Colcha	**COAL**-cha
Cabinet	Gabinete	ga-b-**NAY**-tay

English	Español	Guide
Chair	Silla	**SEE**-ya
Clock	Reloj	**RAY**-low
Closet	Armario	are-**MAR**-e-oh
Curtain	Cortina	cor-**T**-na
Desk	Escritorio	es-cree-**TOR**-ree-oh
Door	Puerta	pooh-**AIR**-ta
Dust ruffle	Guardapolvo	goo-**ARE**-da-**POLE**-vo
Floor	Piso	**P**-so
Iron	Plancha	**PLAHN**-cha
Ironing board	Tabla de planchar	**TA**-blah de plan-**CHAR**
Lamp	Lámpara	**LAMB**-pa-rah
Light	Luz	loose
Mirror	Espejo	es-**PAY**-jo
Pillow	Almohada	al-mo-**HA**-da
Pillow case	Funda de almohada	**FOON**-da day al-mo-**HA**-da
Sheet	Sábano	**SA**-baa-no
Shower	Ducha	**DO**-cha
Sink	Lavabo	la-**VA**-bow
Sofa	Sofá	so-**FA**
Table	Mesa	**MAY**-sa
Telephone	Teléfono	tay-**LAY**-foe-no
Television	Televisión	tay-lay-v-see-**ON**
Trash	Basura	bah-**SUE**-rah

English	Español	Guide
Towel	Toalla	toe-EYE-ya
Wall	Pared	pah-RED
Water	Agua	AH-gua
Window	Ventana	ven-TAN-na

Tips & Tidbits

Latin Americans can be skilled diplomats who are sensitive to the world around them. Conversation is seen as an important skill and discussions are often lively. Culturally, Latin Americans prefer to avoid confrontation whenever possible to avoid the loss of face for themselves or others. Striving to reach a consensus where there are no winners or losers is an important goal in any conflict. Saving face is so important that many Latinos are highly sensitive to criticism and take it personally — even on the job. If you are a manager, it's essential that you realize this tendency and make every effort to avoid situations which show your Latino employees in a less than positive light especially in front of others.

Around the Property
Alrededor de la Propiedad

Resorts, hotels and apartment complexes are full of interesting spaces for guests and residents to enjoy. Many times attractions are the reasons visitors choose these locations for relaxation or business conferences — or even a place to live. These amenities, although they are beautiful, may require considerable maintenance. Keeping the grounds in top shape requires working with large numbers of trained professionals. How many of the following spots or items do you have on your property?

English	Español	Guide
Bar	Bar	bar
Beach	Playa	**PLY**-ya
Courtyard	Patio	**PA**-t-oh
Exit light	Luz de salida	loose day sa-**LEE**-da
Fire detector	Detector de fuego	day-tek-**TOR** day foo-**A**-go
Fountain	Fuente	foo-**N**- tay
Game room	Salón de juegos	sa-**LAWN** day who-**WAY**-goes
Garden	Jardín	har-**DEAN**
Garden path	Andador	an-da-**DOOR**
Golf course	Campo de golf	**CAM**-po day golf
Guest room	Habitación	ah-b-ta-see-**ON**
Laundry	Lavandería	la-van-dare-**REE**-ah
Lawn	Césped	**SAYS**-ped
Lobby	Vestíbulo	vase-**T**-boo-la
Maintenance shop	Taller	ta-**YER**
Office	Oficina	oh-fee-**SEEN**-na
Parking lot	Estacionamiento	es-ta-see-on-a-me-**N**-toe
Pool	Piscina

Alberca | p-**SEEN**-na

al-**BEAR**-ca |
Restaurant	Restaurante	ray-sta-our-**RANT**-tay
Smoke detector	Detector de humo	day-tec-**TOR** day **OO**-mo
Storeroom	Almacén	al-ma-**SIN**
Tennis court	Cancha de tenis	**CAN**-cha day **TAY**-knees

Giving Directions

The ability to give directions in *español* is one of the most practical skills you can have. It adds to your conversational ability and it's a skill you will use over and over again. Slowly, you can start to learn this important vocabulary by knowing simple things, such as the four directions: north, south, east, and west. Then, add turns like right and left. Before you know it, you'll be able to give directions to places around town and in your office. This practical vocabulary is easy to practice because you can work on it anywhere you go!

English	Español	Guide
Where is…?	¿Dónde está…?	DON-day es-TA
North	Norte	NOR-tay
South	Sur	SUE-er
East	Este	ES-tay
West	Oeste	oh-ES-tay
Above	Encima	n-SEE-ma
Aisle	Pasillo	pa-SEE-yo
Avenue	Avenida	ah-ven-KNEE-da
Behind	Detrás	day-TRAHS
Down	Abajo	ah-BAA-ho
Here	Aquí	ah-KEY
In front of	En frente de	n FREN-tay day
Inside	Adentro	ah-DEN-tro
Near	Cerca	CER-ca
Next to	Al lado de	al LA-doe day

English	Español	Guide
Outside	Afuera	ah-foo-AIR-ah
Over there	Allá	ah-YA
Straight ahead	Adelante	ah-day-LAN-tay
Street	Calle	ca-YEA
There	Allí	ah-YE
To the left	A la izquierda	ah la ees-key-AIR-dah
Turn	Doble	DOE-blay
To the right	A la derecha	ah la day-RAY-cha
Up	Arriba	ah-REE-ba

Around Town

Spanish-speaking families are traveling more and more on their vacations. Family destinations like Orlando, Las Vegas and beach resorts are common choices. If you are working at the reception desk, guests will ask you a wide variety of questions. You need to know where restaurants are located, transportation options are available and be able to help with financial arrangements such as the locations of banks or automatic teller machines. When a Hispanic family checks in to your property, they will want to visit the surrounding area too. Knowing vocabulary for places around town will provide you with the kind of terminology that will make you a good ambassador for your community.

The next time you go out to run check the list below. Where are you going? Make a numbered list of the places you intend to go along with the Spanish words for the directions that will get you there. Now you can practice three important sets of vocabulary at the same time. Now, let's get going!

English	Español	Guide
Airport	Aeropuerto	ah-eh-row-poo-AIR-toe
Automatic teller machine	Cajera automática	a-HAIR-rah ow-toe-MAH-t-ca
Bakery	Panadería	pan-ah-day-REE-ah
Bank	Banco	BAN-co
Barber shop	Peluquería	pay-loo-kay-REE-ah
Beauty salon	Salón de belleza	sa-LAWN day bay-YEA-sa
Church	Iglesia	e-GLAY-see-ah
City hall	Municipio	moon-knee-SEE-p-oh
Fire department	Departamento de bomberos	day-par-ta-MEN-toe day bom-BAY-rows
Florist	Florería	floor-ray-REE-ah
Gas station	Gasolinera	gas-so-lee-NAY-rah
Grocery store	Grosería	gros-eh-REE-ah
Hospital	Hospital	os-p-TAL
Hotel	Hotel	oh-TEL
Jewelry store	Joyería	hoy-eh-REE-ah
Laundromat	Lavandería	la-van-day-REE-ah
Library	Biblioteca	b-blee-oh-TECK-ah
Market	Mercado	mare-CA-doe
Movie theatre	Cine	SEEN-nay
Museum	Museo	moo-SAY-oh
Park	Parque	PAR-kay
Pharmacy	Farmacia	far-MA-see-ah
Police station	Estación de policía	es-ta-see-ON day po-lee-SEE-ah

English	Español	Guide
Post office	Correo	core-**A**-oh
Restaurant	Restaurante	res-tower-**AHN**-tay
School	Escuela	es-coo-**A**-la
Shoe store	Zapatería	sa-pa-tay-**REE**-ah
Store	Tienda	t-**N**-da
Super market	Super mercado	soo-**PEAR** mare-**CA**-doe
Theatre	Teatro	tay-**AH**-trow
Train station	Estación de tren	es-ta-see-**ON** day tren
Subway	Metro	**MAY**-tro

CHEVROLET NOVA

Tips & Tidbits:

Neither the names of businesses nor the names of streets are translated into Spanish. The proper name of your company is its brand or trade-mark and should not be translated. Consequently, the name of a street is its proper or given name and should not be translated either.

In most Latin American cities, numbers and the words street and avenue are commonly used in addresses as they are in most metropolitan areas of the US. It's not uncommon to find 5th Avenue or 52nd Street. But, our neighborhood streets...well, that's another story entirely! Street names like Taniger Lane, Red Fox Run, or Wood Stork Cove are impossible to translate from one language to another. You should be aware, however, that sometimes a Spanish-speaking person will give you the number of their street address *en español*. Simple numbers are one of the most important sets of vocabulary you can have!

Calming Customers — Calmando Clientes

Building a good relationship with Latino customers is what good customer service is all about. The path to starting that relationship often begins with a smile and a simple phrase or two. When you speak Spanish to your Latino customers, you send a message to them that they are important to you and that you appreciate their business. On the following list you will find some great "one-liners" that will help you get started. Talking to parents about their children is a great way to start. Practice these often and have fun! You should get lots of smiles and encouragement from everyone!

English	Español	Guide
Don't worry.	No se preocupe.	no say pray-oh-**COO**-pay
Good luck!	¡Buena suerte!	boo-**WAY**-na **SWEAR**-tay
Calm down	¡Cálmese!	**CAL**-may-say
How pretty!	¡Qué bonito! (m)	kay bow-**KNEE**-toe
	¡Qué bonita! (f)	kay bow-**KNEE**-ta
He's precious!	¡Es precioso!	es pray-see-**OH**-so
She's precious!	¡Es preciosa!	es pray-see-**OH**-sa
What a smile!	¡Qué sonrisa!	kay son-**REE**-sa
Have a nice day!	Tenga un buen día.	**TEN**-ga oon boo-**WAYNE** D-ah
How old is your baby?	¿Cuántos años tiene su bebé?	coo-**AN**-toes **AH**-nyos t-**N**-a sue bay-**BAY**
What's your baby's name?	¿Cómo se llama su bebé?	**CO**-mo say **YA**-ma sue bay-**BAY**

One for the Road: Phrases to Use Any Time

Obviously, conversation is made up of more than just lists of words. It will take practice and determination for you to achieve free-flowing conversation in a language that's new to you. Learning Spanish is a slow and steady process for adults. It could take several months before you begin to "think" in Spanish, so don't expect to achieve native speaker speed overnight. There will be times when you feel like you can't remember anything you've studied. That's natural. It happens to everyone. Try not to be discouraged. The rewards you'll receive from learning to speak Spanish are far greater than a little bit of frustration. If you keep working, it won't be long before you'll have a breakthrough. Learning Spanish is a lot like eating a great steak. You don't want to rush it. Cut each bite of your Spanish, chew it over carefully and savor each morsel. Moving along at a slower pace will help you retain what you learn longer.

Spanish is a language that has loads of zest and flair. It is punctuated with single words and short phrases that can really express a lot of sentiment. The next time you have an opportunity to observe native speakers, listen carefully. You may hear them switch from English to Spanish, depending on what they are saying. And, you might hear them use any of the "one-liners" listed below. Phrases like these add spice to your conversation. Use the following list to help you take your conversational skills to the next level.

English	Español	Guide
Are you sure?	¿Está seguro? (a)	es-TA say-GOO-row
Excellent!	¡Excelente!	x-say-LENT-tay
Fantastic!	¡Fantástico!	fan-TAS-t-co
Good idea.	Buena idea.	boo-A-na e-DAY-ah
Happy birthday!	¡Feliz cumpleaños!	fay-LEASE coom-play-AH-nyos

English	Español	Guide
Have a nice day.	Tenga un buen día.	**TEN**-ga un boo-**WAYNE** **DEE**-ah
I agree.	De acuerdo.	day ah-coo-**AIR**-doe
I believe so.	Creo que sí.	**CRAY**-oh kay **SEE**
I'm so glad.	Me alegro.	may ah-**LAY**-gro
I'll be right back.	¡Ahora vengo!	ah-**OR**-ah **VEIN**-go
I'm leaving now.	¡Ya me voy!	ya may **VOY**
That's OK.	Está bien.	es-**TA** b-**N**
It's important.	Es importante.	es eem-pour-**TAHN**-tay
It's serious.	Es grave.	es **GRA**-vay
It's possible.	Es posible	es po-**SEE**-blay
Like this?	¿Así?	ah-**SEE**
Maybe.	Quizás.	key-**SAHS**
Me, neither	Yo tampoco.	yo tam-**PO**-co
Me, too	Yo también.	yo tam-b-**N**
More or less	Más o menos.	mas oh **MAY**-nos
Really?	¿De veras?	day **VER**-ahs
Sure	¡Claro!	**CLA**-row
That depends.	Depende.	day-**PEN**-day
We'll see you.	Nos vemos.	nos **VAY**-mos

Tips & Tidbits

Use short phrases to spice up your conversation. Start with one phrase per week and see how many different situations you can occur where you can use your "phrase of the week."

Typing in Spanish on Your Computer
Inserting Letters with Shortcut Keys

When you need to type letters with accent marks or use Spanish punctuation, you will use keys that you have probably never used before! Actually, you are *composing characters* using the **control** key. It is located on the bottom row of keys. You will see that it is such an important key that there is one on both sides. It keeps the computer from moving forward one space so that the accent goes on *top* of the letter instead of *beside* it.

Always remember to hold the control key down first. It will be the *key* to your success in word processing Spanish. With a little practice these keys will become a normal part of your word processing skills.

Also, if using MS Word, you may use the menu command Insert>Symbol.

To insert	For a PC, Press	For a Mac, Press
á, é, í, ó, ú, ý Á, É, Í, Ó, Ú, Ý	CTRL+' (APOSTROPHE), *the letter*	OPTION + e, *the letter*
â, ê, î, ô, û Â, Ê, Î, Ô, Û	CTRL+SHIFT+^ (CARET), *the letter*	OPTION + i, *the letter*
ã, ñ, õ Ã, Ñ, Õ	CTRL+SHIFT+~ (TILDE), *the letter*	OPTION + n, *the letter*
ä, ë, ï, ö, ü, ÿ Ä, Ë, Ï, Ö, Ü, Ÿ	CTRL+SHIFT+: (COLON), *the letter*	OPTION + u, *the letter*
¿	ALT+CTRL+SHIFT+?	OPTION+SHIFT+ ?
¡	ALT+CTRL+SHIFT+!	OPTION + !

Basic Information
Please Print

Date: _____

　　　　　　　　　　　　　　　　　Month　　Day　　Year

Mr.
Mrs.
Miss_____

　　　First Name　　　*Middle Name*　　*Paternal Surname*　　*Maternal Surname*
(Husband)

Address:_____

　　　　　　　　　　　　　　　　　Street

_____

　　　City　　　　　　　　　*State*　　　　　　　*Zip Code*

Telephone: Home _____　　Work_____

　　　　　　Cell_____　　Fax _____

Email Address: _____

Social Security Number: _____-_____-_____　　Date of birth: _____
　　　　　　　　　Month　　Day　　Year

Driver's License Number: _____

Occupation: _____

Place of employment: _____

Marital Status:　　☐　Married　　☐　Divorced
　　　　　　　　☐　Single　　☐　Separated
　　　　　　　　☐　Widow

Husband's name: _____
　　　　First Name　　*Middle Name*　*Paternal Surname*　*Maternal Surname (Husband)*

Wife's name: _____
　　　First Name　*Middle Name*　　*Paternal Surname*　*Maternal Surname　(Husband)*

In case of emergency: _____　Telephone: _____

Signature: _____　Date: _____

Practicing What You Have Learned

Practice is an important part of the language learning process. The more you include practice in your daily routine, the more comfortable and fluent you will become.

The key to practicing Spanish is to set realistic goals. Don't let the language learning process become overwhelming to you. Yes, there is a lot to learn, and it will take some time. But, by setting realistic goals, you have a greater chance of sticking with it. Each of us has different learning styles, so find out what works best for you and break the material down into small pieces. Some of us learn best by listening. Others need to write the words and phrases in order to visualize them. Generally the more of your senses that you involve in the learning process, the faster you will retain the information. Focus and practice one thing at a time. It's doing the little things that will make the greatest difference in the long run. Working five minutes every day on your Spanish is *mucho* better than trying to put in an hour of practice time only once each week. Consistency in your practice is critical.

Here are some practice tips that have worked for me and others who have participated in *SpeakEasy's Survival Spanish*™ training programs over the last few years.

1. Start practicing first thing in the morning. The shower is a great place to start. Say the numbers or run through the months of the year while you wash your hair. If you practice when you start your day you are more likely to continue to practice as the day progresses.

2. Use your commute time to practice. Listening to CDs, music and Spanish language radio stations will help you get the rhythm of Spanish. It will also increase your vocabulary.

3. If you are stopped in traffic, look around you for numbers on billboards or the license tags of the cars in front of you to help you practice. Don't just sit there—do something!

4. Investigate sites on the internet. Sites such as www.about.spanish.com and www.studyspanish.com are great places to practice and to learn, not to mention the fact that they are free!

5. Buy Spanish magazines or pick up Spanish newspapers that are published in your area. Many magazines like *People* have Spanish versions and almost every community in the country has a Spanish language newspaper or two. Many of them are free.

6. If there aren't any Spanish newspapers in your area, you can find a variety of publications from Latin America on the internet. Major cities in Latin America all have newspapers that are easy to find on-line.

7. Practice as often as possible, even five minutes a day will help.

8. Don't give up! You didn't learn English overnight and you won't learn Spanish that way either. Set realistic goals and don't go too far too fast.

9. Learn five to ten words each week.

10. Practice at work with a friend.

11. Read! These books will make great additions to your library.

Baez, Francia and Chong, Nilda. *Latino Culture*. Intercultural Press, 2005

Einsohn, Marc and Steil, Gail. *The Idiot's Guide to Learning Spanish on Your Own*. Alpha Books, 1996

Hawson, Steven R. *Learn Spanish the Lazy Way*. Alpha Books, 1999.

Reid, Elizabeth. Spanish *Lingo for the Savvy Gringo*. In One Ear Publications, 1997

Wald, Susana. *Spanish for Dummies.* Wiley Publishing, 2000.

About the Author

Myelita Melton, MA

Myelita Melton, founder of SpeakEasy Communications, remembers the first time she heard a "foreign" language." She knew from that moment what she wanted to do with her life. "Since I was always the kid in class that talked too much," Myelita says, "I figured it would be a good idea to learn more than one language—that way I could talk to a lot more people!" After high school, she studied in Mexico at the *Instituto de Filológica Hispánica* and completed both her BA and MA in French and Curriculum Design at Appalachian State University.

"Lita's" unique career includes classroom instruction and challenging corporate experience. She has won several national awards, including a prestigious *Rockefeller* scholarship. In 1994 she was named to *Who's Who Among Outstanding Americans*. Myelita's corporate experience includes owning a television production firm, working with NBC's Spanish news division, *Canal de Noticias,* and Charlotte's PBS affiliate WTVI. She continues to broadcast with WDAV, a National Public Radio affiliate near Lake Norman in North Carolina where she lives.

In 1997 Myelita started SpeakEasy Communications to offer industry-specific Spanish instruction in North Carolina. The company is now the nation's leader in Spanish training, offering thirty of *SpeakEasy's Survival Spanish*™ programs and publications to companies, associations, and colleges throughout the US.

Lita is also a member of the National Speaker's Association and the National Council for Continuing Education and Training. Many of her clients say she is the most high-energy, results-oriented speaker they have ever seen. As she travels the country speaking on cultural diversity issues in the workplace and languages, she has truly realized her dream of being able to talk to the world.